095903

CANTERBURY COLLEGE
NEW DOVER ROAD, CANTERBURY
LEARNING RESOURCES
CENTRE

D0754859

CROWOOD SPORTS GUIDES

BADMINTON

TECHNIQUE • TACTICS • TRAINING

John Edwards

The Carey Centre
Canterbury College
New Dover Road
Canterbury, Kent CT1 3AJ

CLASS No. ...796.345.EDW

BOOK No. ....095903........

LOAN PERIOD...1w...........

SHELF ....lending.........

DELETED

Canterbury College

095903

First published in 1997 by
The Crowood Press Ltd
Ramsbury, Marlborough
Wiltshire SN8 2HR

www.crowood.com

This impression 2005

© The Crowood Press Ltd 1997

All rights reserved. No part of this publication may be reproduced or transmitted in any form or by any means, electronic or mechanical, including photocopy, recording, or any information storage and retrieval system, without permission in writing from the publishers.

British Library Cataloguing-in-Publication Data

A catalogue record for this book is available from the British Library.

ISBN 1 86126 027 X

Acknowledgements
The author and publishers would like to thank the following for their help in the production of this book: Stephen Line (for photographs); The Badminton Association of England (for the use of their courts); Alison Drage, Miles Green, Ian Stockford, Rachel Harrison (Northamptonshire Juniors) and Clive Ellames (Director of Development, Badminton Association of England).

Dedication
To my wife Jennie, with grateful thanks for her patience and consideration during the production of this book.

Note: In March 2005 the Badminton Association of England was rebranded as BADMINTON England.

Unless specific reference is made within the book, the pronouns 'he', 'him' and 'his' are used in contexts intended to apply to both male and female players.

It has been assumed that the reader is a right-handed player.

Typeset by Annette Findlay/Image Engineers, Wiltshire
Printed and bound by Times Publishing Group, Malaysia

CONTENTS

PREFACE

Badminton is easy to play – a bold statement but one that is true. All you need is the ability to hit upwards and downwards and you have the components of a simple rally!

The game has many attractions. It can be enjoyed by all ages, as an individual or as a part of a team or family, courts are usually available in most places, and whether you have ample spare time or little to spare you can set your own commitment levels and play socially or competitively. Add to this that the singles game differs greatly from the doubles game and you have the ingredients of a sport that is easy to learn, fascinating and infectious.

Its exact origins are unknown and accounts do vary. However, it is played all over the world and has been in existence for many decades. Many believe that a crude form of the game was first played at Badminton, the Gloucestershire estate of the Duke of Beaufort, in the 1860s. Others claim that it was first played in India. The first organized body for the sport was the Badminton Association of England, formed in 1934.

Throughout Britain, the game is enjoyed by a some five million people, who play in a variety of venues. Though some courts remain in church and village halls, the majority of players gain their enjoyment using the leisure centres that have become so prolific.

Badminton is an interesting challenge for both the newcomer to the game and the seasoned player. The starting point is to master the techniques required to move around the court and strike the shuttle. In tandem with this you will need to find ways to out-think your opponents, exploit weaknesses, play to your strengths and apply psychology. You may develop a particular flair for singles, level or mixed doubles or become a player who is fortunate enough to be equally at home in all three – and you will never stop learning.

The aim of this book is to improve your performance and understanding of this great game. Whether you are a newcomer, established player or coach, I hope that the contents stimulate thought and contribute to your enjoyment of the sport.

PART 1
INTRODUCTION
TO BADMINTON

CHAPTER 1

THE LAWS OF THE GAME

Players should familiarize themselves with the complete laws of badminton. These are published by the International Badminton Federation (IBF) and are available from the Badminton Association of England. This chapter contains a simplified summary for those new to the game.

Badminton can be played between two people (singles) or four (doubles). The aim is to hit the shuttlecock (more usually referred to as a 'shuttle' or sometimes as a 'bird') over the net and into play in such a manner that it either hits the ground before your opponent can reach it, or your opponent hits the shuttle out of court or into the net. The shuttle may not bounce at any time during the rally and you can only gain points by winning the rally that starts with your service. There are five disciplines in badminton: Ladies' and Men's Singles, Ladies' and Men's Doubles, and Mixed Doubles. There are several methods of scoring. Matches are normally the best of three games to 11 or 15 points, but in some tournaments matches can consist of the best of three games to 7 points or one game to 21 points.

In the singles game, the server's score is always called first and zero is referred to as 'love'. When the server's score in the singles game is an even number, he must serve from the right-hand service court area; when his score is an odd number he must serve from the left. The service must be directed into the diagonally opposite service court area and his opponent must stand within this area. A player can only score a point if he wins the rally on his serve. If he wins the first rally having served from the right-hand service court, the score

Fig 1   The umpire checks that the height of the net in the centre is exactly 5ft (1.524m).

becomes 1–0 and he would then serve from the left court and so on.

In IBF tournaments in Ladies' Singles, Ladies' Doubles and Mixed Doubles the player or team who gains 11 points first wins the game. If the score reaches 10 all, the receiver can choose to play either straight through to 11 points or to 'set'. If the option to 'set' is chosen the winner will be the player or team who first gains 3 points, thereby taking the score to 13.

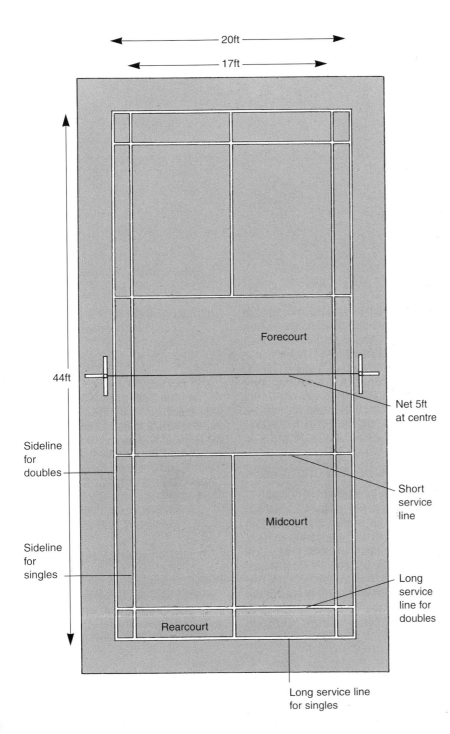

Fig 2   The layout of a badminton court.

USEFUL TIP – SCORING IN DOUBLES

The player who serves at the start of any game will serve from or receive in the right service court when his team's score is love or an even number. This tip also applies to the player who receives at the start of any game.

In Men's Singles and Men's Doubles, the player or team who gain 15 points first wins the game. If the score reaches 14 all, the receiver can choose to play either straight through to 15 points or to 'set'. If the option to 'set' is chosen the winner will be the player or team who gains 3 points, thereby taking the score to 17 points. The Badminton Association of England and its affiliated counties have chosen to play Ladies' Singles only to 11 points and the remaining disciplines to 15 points.

When playing doubles, at the start of each game only one player serves. If he wins the rally he serves again from the left-hand court and so on until he loses the rally and the service passes to the opposing team. After this both members of the side serving serve in turn. Each time a team gains the right to serve, the first service is always delivered from the right-hand service court. The serve must be returned by the receiver who must stand within the diagonally opposite service court; thereafter the shuttle can be hit by either player into any area of their opponents' court.

When serving, the shuttlecock must be hit with an underarm action from a position below the waist. Some part of the server's and receiver's feet must remain in contact with the ground until the shuttle is struck by the server.

CHAPTER 2

GETTING STARTED – CLOTHING, EQUIPMENT AND FOOTWEAR

There is every possibility that you already possess suitable clothing and footwear to play badminton and that your only concern lies with the acquisition of a racket and shuttles. Indeed you may even find that these items are also in your possession – gathering dust in the attic – following a brief experiment with the game on the beach or in the garden some years ago. If so, you can be playing badminton in no time.

Initially, while you explore the rudiments of the game, you may consider hiring a racket from your local leisure centre or borrowing one from a friend. If you choose to play regularly, however, there is no substitute for being in possession of your own racket, wearing suitable clothing and using footwear that will help you cope with the demands of the game and the surface of the court you play on.

Clothing

If you are a newcomer to the game of badminton playing within a leisure or sports complex you can wear whatever clothing you wish. Ideally, though, you should opt for loose fitting items that allow freedom of movement and let the body 'breathe' naturally as you engage in physical activity. Where the game is played indoors, you often sweat and it is advisable to wear clothing made of a material that absorbs perspiration and is easily washed and dried.

This casual approach to clothing is fine for the social player enjoying a game with friends, but once you join an organized club the situation may well change. Here you will encounter your first taste of etiquette and clothing regulations. Until you reach county standard, there are no hard and fast rules but you will find that established league clubs prefer, or even insist on, the wearing of recognized sports clothing. Some clubs stipulate that items must be predominantly white, others do not. If you are in doubt the best advice is to ask the club secretary on joining or visiting for the first time.

Once you join a club or become involved in league play you will, at the very least, need to buy more shirts! By now you could have progressed from the casual player who enjoyed an hour once or twice a week to the fanatic who tries not to miss a minute of a three hour club night and in addition finds himself in one, two or even more club teams playing in leagues.

Badminton is an explosive game with heavy demands placed on the feet. You owe it to yourself to feel comfortable, so choose your socks with care. The cheapest are not always the best. If you are prone to blisters do take your time when purchasing and avoid socks with raised and abrasive seams. Remember also that because sports socks are often thicker than normal socks it is advisable to wear your sports socks when choosing your badminton footwear.

Tracksuits are a most useful, almost essential part of your kit and there is a wide variety of choice. These items are worn to and from the sports hall and during the warm up prior to actual play. They are particularly beneficial during intervals between matches as they help to keep the limbs warm and supple.

Unless the hall is especially warm, you should wear your tracksuit during the pre-match knock up and remove it before the match commences. Some club and tournament regulations insist that tracksuits are removed for match play. You would be well advised to select a tracksuit that has a zipped bottom to the legs so that you can slip out of the trousers easily without having to remove your shoes.

Rackets

Your racket is the most important purchase you will make, so the process should not be rushed and is best carried out during the close season after your serious league play has finished. Furthermore it is during out-of-season times that shops and department stores have their sales and many a bargain can be found. You will need to consider cost, durability, weight and balance, stringing, tension and grip size.

Cost

As there are so many different types of racket and prices vary greatly it is difficult to generalize. However, as with other racket sports, you get what you pay for. As badminton strings are of narrow gauge, breakages are far more common than in squash and tennis. For this reason, if your resources permit, it is advisable to have two identical rackets.

Choosing a racket is not easy. The commercial world is one of change and marketing agencies are quick to introduce new ideas and gimmicks to secure your attention. Cheap rackets with poor quality strings may look good and feel fine within the confines

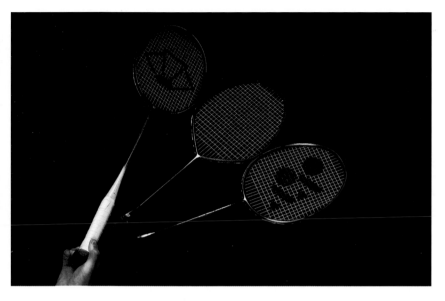

Fig 3 Three of the many types of racket on the market today. From left to right: parallel head shape, Y–joint axis and isometric box shape

Weight and Balance

Many players prefer light, perfectly balanced rackets to increase manoeuvrability and speed of racket recovery after playing a stroke. By comparison others enjoy the feel of a racket that, though light overall, is head heavy because they maintain it enables them to produce more power into their play. It really is a matter of personal preference and you may well have to experiment to find what suits you.

You can establish if a racket is balanced or head heavy by balancing the shaft horizontally on the forefinger. If the distance between the finger and the end of the head of the racket is less than the opposite side, then the racket is head heavy. A light racket will weigh in the region of 80 to 100g.

Stringing

The majority of rackets come ready strung, giving you no say in the type to be used and the tension applied. You will be amazed at the large range of stringing that is available to you and the lack of advice in terms of string quality and tension. Usually the more expensive the racket the better the quality of the string and the design used to incorporate the string within the frame. You need to make sure that the racket has grommets – plastic guards or sleeves that protrude through the holes in the frame – and where the string sits outside the frame It lies within in a channel or groove that is below the rim of the frame.

Pure gut is more resilient and can withstand greater tension than strings of a synthetic texture, but you will rarely, if ever, see a gut strung racket in a shop. Once again, technology plays its part in the market and any claim regarding the durability of badminton string must be weighed against two very important facts – badminton string is of a narrow gauge

of the shop but you may well find that they do not last long during regular play.

The racket you choose must be right for you both physically and mentally. Some suppliers will allow you to try out rackets on court before you finally decide, and if you are fortunate enough to be offered this opportunity you should take it.

Durability

When considering durability you will be moving into a world of high technology. Rackets made up of materials such as steel, aluminium, kevlar, boron, and ceramic fibre will be made available to you. You may

encounter graphite composite rackets made up of a mixture of more than one material and rackets where the shaft is made of a material that is completely different from that used for the head.

You will be able to compare one-piece rackets against those with a separately constructed head. It is no easy process. You will undoubtedly find yourself caught in the dilemma that the lighter the racket, the better it will feel but the more expensive it will be! You will also find that the lighter and more expensive the racket, the less likely it will be to stand up to a clash with your doubles partner or a bang on the ground.

Schools and institutions, where economy plays a major part in choice, will best be served by rackets made up of metal construction, such as aluminium, but these rackets do weigh a lot more than those produced from Kevlar and boron. Whichever racket you choose, where durability is concerned, look after it, treat it with care but do not expect it to last for ever.

KIT CHECK

Club nights can be busy. Know the position of your racket both on and off court! When not playing, stow your racket away until required.

and no player can guarantee always to hit the shuttle in the centre of the racket face!

Synthetic strings are likely to outlast those made of gut and if you keep the mishits to a minimum you will enjoy value for money with any string made of a multi-filament construction. In this process numerous fibres are bonded together within an outer shell to create a tremendously strong product that can be manufactured in a variety of gauges and colours.

Tension

Good quality pre-strung rackets are usually strung to a tension of between 14 and 19lb but most rackets are capable of withstanding tensions of around 23 to 24lb. When considering what tension is best for you, do not be misled into thinking that more power is produced by tighter strings. If you increase the tension of the strings you create a smaller 'sweet spot' on the racket face and should enjoy more control but less power. Conversely, a reduction in the tension of the strings increases the elasticity of the mesh bed, enlarges the 'sweet spot' and while power is increased a small percentage of control is sacrificed.

> **KEY POINT**
>
> When buying a racket the string is a fundamentally important part of the package but it is the performance of the frame that dictates the price. Do not forget to consider the type of string and the tension to be applied.

Grip Size

Although rackets are manufactured in four sizes it has become customary for them to be purchased by the retailer in only two. The size relates to the circumference of the grip and it is most important to consider this aspect when purchasing your racket. Too small a grip will result in your holding the racket far too tightly and could even cause tennis elbow (a painful inflammation of the tendons). In addition, an incorrect grip size could inhibit the full range of wrist movement and have an adverse effect on the quality of some of your strokes. The two most common grip sizes are 3½ and 3⅝.

Before choosing your grip size remember that racket handles are made of wood. Therefore, while you can easily make the handle of a racket larger by applying purpose made grips made of a towelling or tape material, you would have considerable difficulty reducing the size.

Shuttles

Initially you will not appreciate the degree of importance that ought to be applied to the selection of your shuttles. Shuttles are yet another item that have secured the full attention of the market, the inevitable result being that numerous different makes are available to you at varied cost. While numerous manufacturers exist, it is possible to categorize shuttles into only two types – feather and non-feather. What then is the difference and what factors will effect your choice?

> **KIT CHECK**
>
> Never rely on others to supply the shuttles. Always carry a small quantity in your bag.

Feather Shuttles

Feather shuttles are used in all top national and international events and in the majority of league clubs up and down the UK. New shuttles will fly perfectly and consistently until the feathers are damaged or broken, and on reaching their highest point when hit high and deep to the rearcourt, fall quite steeply towards the floor.

The feathers used in the creation of a shuttle are taken from geese and despite careful construction (mostly by hand) they are fragile, easily damaged and not very durable. As a result of the need to change the shuttle once the flight becomes too poor or its speed is impaired, clubs get through far more feather shuttles than their counterparts who have decided to play with a non-feather equivalent.

Non-feather Shuttles

For the newcomer to the game it is advisable to use non-feather shuttles for reasons of cost. Although nowadays synthetic shuttles are no cheaper to buy than feather shuttles, they are a much more cost-effective purchase because their life is considerably longer. The search for a plastic or synthetic shuttle that matches the flight characteristics of the feathered variety has been going on for years. Poor quality non-feather shuttles tend to have an erratic flight path and on reaching their highest point do not fall towards the floor as steeply as a feather type.

What you should opt for is a shuttle that matches the feather shuttle as far as is technically possible in terms of flight, speed and touch. If you choose a synthetic shuttle with the same cork, leather covered base as a feather shuttle, you will be well on the way to experiencing the same feel, particularly when playing the more delicate touch shots.

Shuttle Speed

Irrespective of which shuttle you use, its speed is important otherwise the game can become farcical. Feather shuttles are manufactured in anything up to twelve different speeds and are categorised by number – 73 (slow) to 85 (fast) or 4.8 (slow) to 5.0 (fast). Synthetic alternatives are often graded slow, medium or fast. Apart from the amount of force applied to the shuttle by the players, the speed they reach inside the hall depends on many things including air resistance, size of hall, temperature and shuttle condition.

To find out if a shuttle is of the correct speed, it should be struck underarm from above the baseline upwards at about 45 degrees so that it flies parallel to the sideline and lands within 9in (23cm) either side of the back doubles service line on the other side of the net.

Footwear

The arrival of the modern day leisure centre has not only increased the number of facilities available to us for badminton, it has also forced the more sensible player and parent into greater thought regarding the selection of suitable footwear. This is because the majority of new local authority and school venues have floors constructed of concrete, or some other similar substance, and have no give in them whatsoever. Consequently the wearing of inadequate footwear in a sport where starting, stopping, jumping, landing and lunging figure prominently will afford little protection to the joints, especially the knees and ankles.

If you intend to become a regular player, it is important that the shoes you select provide adequate protection by way of cushioning and good grip. A little care and forethought when purchasing your footwear will reduce the likelihood of injury now, minimize the amount of heartache

Fig 4   Some of the equipment the sport requires.

KIT CHECK

Some courts are slippery. Keep an old piece of cloth or towel in your bag and reduce the risk of injury by stepping on to a damp cloth between rallies.

USEFUL TIP

You can prolong the life of your badminton shoes considerably by wearing alternative footwear to and from the sports hall.

and pain in the future and even help prolong your playing career.

There are many specialist sports shops that stock purpose made indoor sports footwear. You will need a lightweight shoe with a sole that should have a non-marking, well defined tread to assist with grip. The heel should be rounded to reduce the chance of slipping. The insole should be adequately cushioned and together with the sole of the shoe should act as a shock absorber and reduce the chance of painful shin splints and heel jar. You can also

purchase separate rubber inserts for the whole shoe or just the heel.

The uppers should be of a material that permits the feet to breathe, and while the shoe should be substantial it should also be flexible. Some players drag their toes when playing certain shots; if you fall into this category look for shoes that have protective material incorporated into the front.

Do take your time when considering and choosing this most important item, and replace your shoes as soon as they are past their best.

CHAPTER 3

PLAYING THE GAME

Courts

The keen player should not have too much difficulty finding a court on which to play. However, as there has been a substantial increase in the numbers of people who are taking part in badminton at leisure centres, it is wise to enrol as a member and enjoy the convenience of being able to book your court in advance by telephone.

Most of the new centres in the UK are run by local authorities and some serve as a venue for school sports, opening to the public in the evenings and at weekends only. Within these buildings multi-purpose areas catering for several sports are found. It is not uncommon to find badminton being played on one or two courts with a long curtain separating the remainder of the area in which another sport is being played. Usually being a member of one particular leisure centre qualifies you for membership of several others that are run by the same local authority in other areas close by. The cost of court hire varies and it is worth checking to see whether the centre operates peak and off peak rates.

Some private clubs and schools possess a suitable badminton facility and in the case of clubs, while the initial enrolment fee will be much more than the cost of enlisting at a local authority venue, very often the court hire thereafter will be free.

Clubs

The location of clubs can be found through information centres such as the local library or by contacting regional representatives who will be able to provide you with a contact number for league or County Associations. There are social and competitive clubs throughout the UK that can also provide you with the opportunity to play the game. Usually such clubs utilize courts within a leisure centre or school and there are considerable advantages to be gained by joining one of them.

One advantage of joining a club is cost – over a season it can provide cheaper badminton for you to enjoy. They also provide the opportunity to meet and play with different people and for the competitive player, many clubs run teams in local leagues or engage in friendly matches against other clubs. Teams are grouped into men's, women's, mixed or medley (level doubles and mixed doubles) leagues and the majority are for doubles play only.

Clubs and their members are encouraged to affiliate to the national governing body, the Badminton Association of England, but this is not mandatory unless your club plays within a league that wishes to enter tournaments sanctioned by the BAE or the County Badminton Association. Most clubs generate their income by setting an annual fee, which is determined by a number of factors such as hall cost, cost of shuttles, frequency of club nights and the number of members.

For the younger player, casual badminton is available in many schools and for the aspiring champion who seeks a competitive environment, most English counties operate Schools Associations under the auspices of the English Schools' Badminton Association.

There are many factors to consider when choosing a club; some are more obvious than others. You will be fortunate to find a club that satisfies your every need but if you spend a little time on the selection process you will be able to narrow the list down quite considerably before making the final decision. The following aspects should be considered:

- How much time do you have available?
- What clubs operate at times that suit you?
- Do you wish to play socially or competitively?
- How many teams does the club have and what proportion of the members play in the teams?
- What is the general standard compared to yours?
- How many courts are available?
- How many members does the club have?
- How high is the ceiling in the hall?
- What facilities does the club have, such as showers and refreshments?
- What is the cost of membership and match fees?
- What is the average age of the members?
- Is the club affiliated to the governing body?
- Is the club insured?
- Is coaching available?

Having made your choice and contacted the club secretary it is usual for you to be invited to a number of club nights. If the club is competitive, this can be somewhat daunting because you are most definitely under trial. However do remember that while they are looking at you, so you are scrutinizing them. If the standard initially appears to be too high do not despair because the majority of clubs cater for a wide range of players and the standard varies enormously from the top division to the lower sections.

It is not the end of the world if your first club visit proves to be a disaster because most clubs allow up to three visits before a decision is made. If your ability is lacking, a helpful club secretary will point you in the direction of a club whose standard is more in line with your own and you will soon be enjoying the many benefits associated with club badminton.

Etiquette

Some knowledge of club and court etiquette together with accepted standards of behaviour will serve to add to your enjoyment of the game. Well organized clubs will have some form of constitution or rules – if the secretary does not offer these to you, ask for a copy because it is well worth taking time to browse through them soon after joining the club rather than plunging straight into an embarrassing situation. The rules will cover the everyday running of the club and full details of the club fees and formal meetings should also be listed.

What may well be omitted are some of the 'collective understandings' found within clubs. At first they will seem unimportant to a newcomer. However, these unwritten points, which have been built up by the players over the years, are important and once you become aware of them you will soon see the reasoning behind them. Surprisingly, though some of them relate to the laws of the game, they will not be

found within the laws booklet. Some of the following suggestions may therefore be helpful if you are new to badminton, not playing with an umpire or have just joined a club.

KEY POINT

If it is your turn to pick a doubles game, do not repeatedly ask players who are much better than you to play. More than once will spoil their evening and you will certainly not enjoy it.

- It is your obligation to make the calls regarding what has happened on your side of the net. If you are in no doubt, make the decision quickly and stick to it.
- Likewise it is your opponent's responsibility to make calls concerning his side.
- If you are in doubt regarding a call on your side, say so and ask your opponent (who may have been better placed to see the shuttle land) for his opinion.
- If he is sure, accept his decision, but if you are both uncertain call 'let' and replay the rally.
- Never ask spectators for their opinion or you may become involved in a dispute with a third party. If, as a spectator, you are asked for an opinion as to whether the shuttle was in or out, abstain.
- If you make a mistake accidentally, correct the call immediately.
- When serving, call out the score regularly to minimize the likelihood of a dispute. Should you find yourself unable to agree the score, go back to the last point when you were both in agreement.
- Never walk behind a court when a rally is in progress.
- In mixed doubles remember that the woman does not have to serve first but it is traditional for her to do so.

- Try to abide by any dress or footwear regulations that are imposed.
- In tournaments, unsuitable playing clothing will not be allowed so do take the trouble to find out what is acceptable.
- At the end of the match, shake hands with your opponent or opponents and if playing in a tournament pass the result to the organizer's desk.
- If you wish to take a colleague or relative to play on a club night, check to see if this is permitted. Some clubs do not allow this when a league match is taking place.

DID YOU KNOW?

You can take to court with two rackets! However there are restrictions concerning the size of the racket head.

- At most clubs, matches on club nights are arranged by selecting players from 'the board'. The majority of systems in operation ensure a reasonably quick turnaround, although this will depend largely on the number of courts available and the number of players there on the night. There is no perfect board procedure and people will try to short-circuit the system. Make sure that you know how the board operates and before you accuse anyone of queue jumping, check first because the committee or selectors may well have the right to arrange practice matches for league pairings.
- Remember that at the start and end of the evening the nets and posts have to be put away. Take your turn.
- If you are selected for league fixtures, check to see if it is your turn to provide refreshments and

be punctual as a courtesy to your opponents.

- Acquire a sound basic knowledge of the laws of the game. It is surprising how many experienced players do not know the laws, especially those connected with the serve.

ETIQUETTE

If you hit the shuttle into the net and lose the rally, it is your responsibility to pick it up and pass it to your opponent.

Tournaments

There are very few players who do not rise to the challenge that presents itself when entering into competition and sooner or later the opportunity to enter a tournament will come your way. In any sport where the game becomes a contest to decide a winner, the availability of tournaments, championships, league and club play provides the platform on which you can assess the progress you have made during practice in a non-competitive environment.

In days gone by only a limited number of tournaments existed and because of this many players chose not to enter for fear of embarrassing themselves with an early exit in round one. Today, however, the range of events available is extensive and they cater for all standards of player.

Open Tournaments

As the name implies, these tournaments are usually open to any player and restrictions on the entry, if any, are minimal. As a general rule, such events are usually quite large and in some areas of the UK they are prestigious in their own right and benefit from sponsorship obtained from a variety of sources. Therefore these tournaments attract the better players and when large numbers apply you may have to play in pre-qualifying matches.

Restricted Tournaments

In comparison to open events, restricted tournaments carry some qualifying factors for the potential entrant. For example, players who wish to enter the South West Restricted Under 16 Tournament would need to satisfy the age limitation and reside within the prescribed geographical area.

Handicap Tournaments

These are extremely popular with the badminton enthusiast who is a club player. The majority of county and league committees organize these

Fig 5   The National Indoor Arena in Birmingham hosts the All England Championships.

tournaments annually and it is not unusual to find clubs that devote one or more of their club nights to this popular form of competition. They are enjoyable and emotive! Enjoyable because the aim is to give all players, irrespective of ability, the chance to pit their wits against the better players on an equal footing, and emotive because your destiny is often left in the hands of an organizing committee.

If you become a member of a handicapping committee you will soon find that you will seldom satisfy all of the people all of the time. Your task will be to award or deprive players of points before the game begins. Hence the best player in the club might start with a minus score and a relative newcomer to the game will start, for example, at plus seven.

Plate Events

Fortunately, the modern day tournament organizer usually makes provision for those players who are unlucky enough to lose their first matches.

The events, known as plate events, provide a much needed extra number of matches for players whose first opponent could well have been one of the seeded players. They also provide some consolation in tournaments that carry high entry fees and to those players who have had to travel long distances to the tournament venue.

Round Robins

Quite often this format is used if there is no plate event. Players are placed into groups (usually referred to as 'boxes') within which they play all other players. Once a winner is determined, that player goes forward into a normal knock-out format.

Seeded Players

It is important for tournament organizers to aim to provide events that are enjoyable and attractive to both the player and the spectator. One measure that assists in achieving this aim is the identification of the better players, who are designated as seeds.

The seeding of players minimizes the risk of the best players meeting each other early in the competition and it also helps to group the lesser ability players together within the draw. Obviously an unseeded player is likely to have to play a seeded player eventually, but if the seeding is accurate and the top seeds win through to the later stages of the competition there will be far closer matches.

LAWS CHECK

An umpire shall not overrule the decision of the line judge

Graded Competitions

This is a relatively new introduction and is now used extensively and successfully by the English Schools' Badminton Association. Players are awarded points for reaching certain stages of a tournament and are then graded as Standard, Intermediate or Premier players. Entrants are allowed to play only within the grading applicable to them and this serves to make sure that players are being matched according to standard. Obviously there is incentive to gain sufficient points to be moved into a higher group.

Sponsorship

Sponsorship is one of the many ways available to the parent or player to reduce the cost of participating in sport. It also provides a lifeline to the tournament organizer, who is often faced with the possibility of expenditure for a particular event being way in excess of income. Do not be misled into thinking that sponsorship is available only to the better player or the organizers of large tournaments. Once the aspiring youngster has a notable title to his credit, or participates in a county or regional squad, some form of sponsorship or grant aid may well be available to him.

Similarly, organizers of tournaments, no matter what the status, would be well advised to seek sponsorship in return for some factor that will benefit the donor. The difficulty is knowing what sources are available and how best to apply for them. Sound advice can be obtained from some county and educational authorities together with the English Sports Council and your local authority.

Players seeking sponsorship should apply to racket or equipment manufacturers for what is known as 'terms'. An application form will be forwarded to them for completion and it is at this moment that parents and players appreciate how useful it is to keep a record of their achievements in the tournaments entered. If approved the player will receive goods or discounts on the products they use and for obvious reasons they must undertake to promote the company's goods at every opportunity.

Many firms see their main avenue of promotion to be through coaches rather than players. Coaches who are particularly active can also seek sponsorship and once again it is not the status of the coach that is usually important. Therefore, if you are qualified, you may find that terms will be made available to you in return for your best endeavours to promote the products you are using. Sponsorship contracts for players and coaches usually run for a period of one year.

CHAPTER 4

COACHING AND COACH EDUCATION

If your introduction to this fascinating sport was by means of attendance on a structured course organized by a leisure centre or education authority, you will already by aware of the benefits to be gained from being coached. If your tuition begins earlier rather than later, the chances of bad habits becoming a natural part of your game will be kept to a minimum. That said, there is a surprising resistance, almost apathy, towards coaching – particularly among adults and more especially from the better club players.

There is every advantage to be gained, no matter what your standard, from being observed, analysed and corrected by an observer who can stand back, watch and help. What is important however, is your choice of coach and like every profession there are the good and the not so good! There is no substitute for experience, and there are enough coaches around for you to be selective and find one that can provide the expertise required to help you improve a particular aspect of your game.

If you are lucky enough to have a coach within your club he will be more than willing to advise you briefly during a club night. But do remember that he is probably there to play and it would be unfair to command a large portion of his time on a club evening.

It may well be better for you to attend a coaching course away from the club; these are often known as 'personal performance courses' and quite often they are organized by your County Badminton Association.

USEFUL TIP – FOR COACHES

Never assume that others know what you mean – always explain yourself fully.

BADMINTON England also arrange residential coaching courses that span a weekend or longer at various venues around the UK. These are good value for money because not only do they cater for different playing standards, you have a prolonged period of time being coached and also have the chance to meet and socialize with other players from all over the UK.

Many players decide to take up coaching in an effort to put something back into a game that has given them so much enjoyment over the years. The more experienced you are as a player the more comfortable you will feel imparting knowledge to others. However, this does not mean that you have to be getting on in years to qualify as a coach – the first recognized Governing Body coaching award, the Level 1 Assistant Coach, can be gained by any person who is over sixteen years of age.

As long as you are aware of your own limitations and restrict your coaching to ability groups that suit your standard as a coach and player, there is nothing to stop you qualifying as a coach at an early age. If you are ever in doubt regarding your ability, the key word to apply to your self-evaluation as a coach is *credibility*. Lose credibility as a coach and you will have problems.

BADMINTON England, working in conjunction with Sports Coach UK has designed an excellent coach education programme to prepare and assess candidates who wish to become qualified as coaches. Full details regarding coach education courses in your area are available from the BADMINTON England website www.badmintonengland.co.uk.

BADMINTON England Courses

Level 1 Assistant Coach Award

This one day course has been designed to give candidates, who must be 16 years of age or over, a good idea of HOW and WHAT to coach to beginner players. It is an ideal first step into coaching for anyone who is interested in helping others to learn how to play safely. Candidates should have some understanding of basic scoring and the laws of the game. Successful candidates will qualify to assist a qualified Coach working with Junior and Senior beginners.

Level 2 Coach Award

This is a three day training course followed by practical and theoretical assessment.   Candidates must have successfully completed the Level 1 Award and be over 18 years of age. On successful completion the candidate will be qualified to coach independently Junior and Senior beginners.

Level 3 Coach Award

This course is currently being designed. When completed full details will be available from BADMINTON England

Teachers Awards

Courses designed specifically for Teachers at Key Stages 1 – 4 are currently being designed. When completed full details will be available from BADMINTON England.

PART 2

SKILLS
AND TECHNIQUES

CHAPTER 5

RACKET GRIP AND HITTING TECHNIQUES

If ever there is a time when the badminton coach needs to be a top class sales representative it is when he is teaching players how to hold the racket. It would be meaningless to simply show or tell the player how to grip the handle without explaining why. The good coach will convey this important aspect by convincing the player that if the correct grip is used at the right time, the chances of producing a successful stroke with the desired outcome will be greatly increased. Furthermore, if the limitations caused by incorrect grip technique are also pointed out, sufficient incentive to master the various correct ways of holding the racket may be achieved.

Grip

You should always remember that the position of the oncoming shuttle – be it straight in front of you or on your racket or non-racket side – is seldom dictated by you. Though you may be able to influence your opponent's choice of shot, or even restrict the number of options available to him, it is he who finally decides. Therefore, you must remain flexible, have the ability to adapt your grip to an ever changing situation and improvise when the occasion demands. Whatever the grip used, control and touch will be increased if the racket is held in the fingers and not within the palm of the hand.

The Forehand Grip

This is the most common of all the grips used in the game. From this basic but effective way of holding the racket changes to other options take place. Using the thumb and forefinger of the non-playing hand hold the racket out in front of you halfway down the shaft so that the handle points towards you. Keep the racket at waist height and make sure that you cannot see any of the strings. Place all the fingers of your racket hand around the handle and your thumb diagonally across the wider segment found on the inside of the handle. You should be lightly shaking hands with the racket.

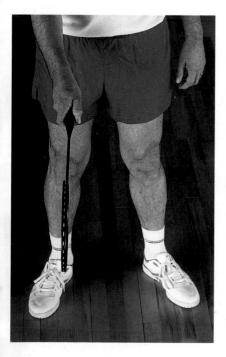

Fig 6   Forehand grip, side view. Note the thumb placed diagonally along the side of the handle.

Fig 7   Forehand grip, frontal view. Note that the racket shaft is in line with the V formed by the thumb and forefinger.

USEFUL TIP

When using the forehand grip imagine you are slapping the shuttle with the palm of your hand. For backhand strokes, consider the racket to be an extension of the thumb.

Fig 8   *Backhand grip, frontal view. The back of the hand is facing the ceiling.*

Check to make sure that you remain unable to see the strings; if the racket were an axe, the blade would be perpendicular and ready to slice downwards if the arm were lowered. Additional checks can now be carried out. First, the V between the thumb and forefinger should be in line with the top bevel of the handle and in line with the shaft. Second, the end of the handle should be resting in the hand just below the thumb. Third, by turning the forearm clockwise and presenting the racket face to the ceiling, if the thumb is lifted off it should reveal that the racket handle is lying in the fingers and not within the palm of the hand.

Failure to adopt this basic grip correctly will result in a restricted range of movement for the racket hand and fingers. As a consequence, there will be limitations in the range of your shots and a profound loss of power in strokes where the whip action is employed. In some cases it will even contribute to the player adopting a stance square to the net, which in turn causes a technically incorrect throwing action and poor forehand overhead strokes.

The Backhand Grip

The correct adoption of this grip will enable you to cope effectively with shuttles on your non-racket side. Hold the racket out in front of you in the forehand grip making sure that you cannot see the strings. Note the position of your thumb, which should be diagonally across the wide segment of the handle. Now using the

Fig 9   *Backhand grip, side view. The thumb is lying flat behind the handle and pointing down the shaft.*

thumb and fingers of your racket hand roll the racket outwards (clockwise) until the thumb is in line with the shaft of the racket and lying flat on top of the wide segment. To check if this has been done correctly, turn the racket arm inwards, as though you were looking at the time on a watch; if your thumbnail is now facing you and the back of your hand is turned up towards the ceiling, all is well.

By turning the racket so that the thumb is behind the handle, greater leverage and power become possible.

The ability to generate power on the non-racket side is especially beneficial when playing shots from the rearcourt. In addition you will also find that you will be able to lock or unlock the hand at the wrist with ease, tilt and turn the racket face at will and with practice achieve greater control and accuracy with your shots.

Grip Variations

Once you become proficient with the forehand and backhand grips you will need to move onwards and learn variations from these two basic methods. There are three reasons why.

First, instances arise during a game when the requirement to adopt a grip variation is forced upon you because no alternative other than to concede exists. Second, there will be times when your position on court is such that a grip change will improve the quality of your selected stroke. Third, some of the placements you choose to make become technically easier to perform if a grip modification is applied.

The Pan Handle Grip

Quite often in both the singles and doubles games the player in the forecourt has the opportunity to hit the shuttle downwards from close to and just above the top of the net. Usually these shots, which are called dabs, are attempted winners. They need to be played crisply from well in front of you and because of this care must be taken not to commit a fault by touching the net or hitting it with your racket. This grip not only enables you to tap the shuttle downwards firmly, but because it inhibits the full wrist movement it restricts the follow through and therefore reduces the likelihood of your racket coming into contact with the net.

To experience the feel of this grip before adopting it during a game, place the racket on the floor with the

Fig 10   Pan handle grip, frontal view. Note the thumb position on the side of the handle pointing upwards.

Fig 11   Pan handle grip, side view. Hand cocked ready to tap the shuttle downwards.

handle towards you. Now pick it up, keeping the strings facing the ground, by wrapping your fingers underneath and around the handle while your thumb remains at the side pointing upwards towards the racket head. Next lift your elbow up so that your racket face is parallel to and just above the top of the net.

During play, the change to this grip from the forehand position is achieved by using the fingers to roll the racket inwards about 90 degrees. Remember that this grip is used only when you are in the forecourt attempting to dab the shuttle downwards. When outside the forecourt, the pan handle grip has no purpose.

The Multi-Purpose Grip

This grip can be used to hit shuttles that are either to the side or directly in front of you. As there is no requirement to change grip, it has obvious advantages. However, the

majority of coaches would agree that this grip is best left to experienced players who possess strong wrists and fingers. Newcomers, and even players with some experience who try using this grip when playing strokes on the non-racket side, find they lose control, accuracy and power. However, it is for you to try and see. Adopt the forehand grip; turn the racket slightly outwards and place your thumb on to the narrow bevel on the handle so that it points directly upwards to the head of the racket.

The Short Grip

For better racket control and more power in quick exchanges played from the midcourt and forecourt areas, move the hand up the racket handle. This variation is particularly useful during the doubles game and has also proved beneficial for players who lack control during the production of a low serve. When using this modification, remember that the

Fig 12   Multi–purpose grip, side view. The thumb is on top of the handle pointing directly towards the head of the racket.

Fig 13   Multi–purpose grip, frontal view.

the basic grip positions – forehand or backhand – still apply.

Hitting Techniques

The method by which you strike the shuttle is called the hitting technique. The different techniques available provide you with the ability to control the head of the racket as contact is made with the shuttle. This control enables you to return the shuttle over the net at slow, medium or fast speed.

If you are unable to perform the different methods of hitting, your game will be severely restricted. At worst you will be restricted to playing all your shots to the midcourt area of your opponent's court. As a beginner, such a limit will not reduce your enjoyment of the game if your opponent is also a newcomer.

However, the moment you face opponents who possess the ability to vary the speed and placement of their shots, the rallies will shorten and your enjoyment level will drop.

Knowledge of the three hitting techniques will help you to address this. Once proficient, you will be able to find ways to gain the initiative and create more winning chances by moving your opponents to all parts of the court. You will play with confidence and flair and eventually introduce an exciting new element into your play – that of deception. Whatever stroke or shot you play, one of three hitting techniques is applied.

The Tap Action

This technique can be used when carrying out strokes on either side of your body or directly in front. Initially cock the hand back at the wrist. As the shuttle is struck, the hand straightens and then returns quickly to the original start position. When the racket face meets the shuttle you should experience a rebound action, similar to that of knocking in a nail, and a sharp, crisp sound is produced.

Fig 14   The short grip in the forehand mode.

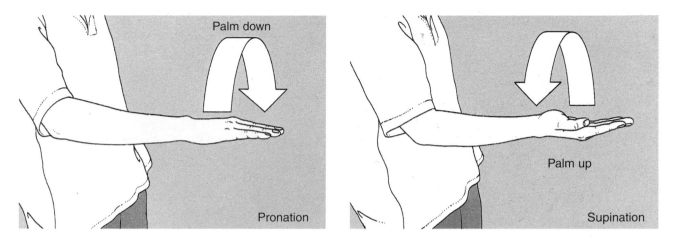

Fig 15   Supination and pronation movements.

The shuttle should travel away from you at medium speed.

The Push Action

Once again this technique can be used with strokes played from all around you. The hand is cocked back and remains locked in to this position throughout the stroke. On contact with the shuttle, a continuous push action is employed and a quiet, dull sound should be heard. The shot is played with the utmost care and the end product should be a shuttle that travels away from you slowly.

The Whip Action

Apart from the backhand cross-court drive, this action is used for strokes played solely on the racket side of your body. The hand is again cocked back at the wrist. The arm swings

quickly through and as the racket makes contact with the shuttle the hand straightens sharply. The shuttle is hit powerfully and travels away at speed. This quick, unrestricted swing produces a follow through phase of the stroke that occurs after hitting the shuttle; the racket arm should continue moving forwards and finish over the non-racket shoulder.

Presenting the Racket Face

In addition to positioning yourself correctly and using the appropriate grip and hitting technique, you will need to understand the mechanics involved in ensuring that the racket face is presented to the shuttle. By twisting the forearm from the elbow the strings of the racket head become available for your overhead or underarm strokes.

If you hold the racket out in front of you in the forehand grip (as in Fig 15) and twist the forearm inwards to turn the palm of the hand down, you will be pronating the forearm from the elbow. If you now take the racket above the head on the racket side of your body you will have opened the racket face for basic forehand overhead strokes. To supinate the forearm you should repeat the process but twist the forearm outwards so that the palm of the hand is turned upwards. Now the racket face will be positioned correctly for underarm strokes such as the forehand net shot and underarm clear. As your strokes develop, these twisting movements will become automatic and with practice you will also learn to vary the degree of the twist to alter the angle of the racket face and play advanced strokes.

CHAPTER 6

MOVEMENT AROUND THE COURT

Top class players never seem to be rushed; they appear to glide almost effortlessly around the court and quite often even have time to spare! For the newcomer the opposite is often the case, with many players charging around the court in uncontrolled fashion with the sole aim of getting to the shuttle as quickly as possible to hit it back over the net. No thought is applied to economy of movement and if some form of balance is maintained it has been achieved by chance.

Some players and coaches believe that because movement is a process that develops naturally during childhood, there is no requirement for it to be taught. Be that as it may, there is much to be gained from knowing and understanding the principles of movement so that you can make the effort necessary to increase efficiency in an area that is already adequate, or improve on a particular weakness that is having an adverse effect on your play.

A vital aspect of good badminton is the ability to move quickly to the shuttle and to hit it from anywhere on the court while you are on balance. You will have a far greater chance of being on balance throughout the rally if your footwork and posture are correct. The sport demands movement forwards, backwards, sideways and diagonally. Add to this a requirement to start and stop quickly at the beginning and end of each movement, and to jump and land on occasions, and you will soon appreciate that some form of controlled application to the subject of movement is essential otherwise you will be leaving much to chance.

Starting

During the game you will discover the need to adopt different stances to help you cope with the situation that is likely to materialise. Which stance is the most suitable depends on the tactical situation and whether you are already slightly in motion or starting from a stationary position, for example receiving the serve. Whatever stance is chosen your ability to move quickly off the mark is essential as you should strive constantly to get to the shuttle early. You can speed up the starting process by analysing how you start and, once the method is identified, improvements can be applied.

Some players keep their legs straight and begin moving by keeping their feet on the ground while they sway off balance until steps are required if only to stop them falling over. This method takes time. Others speed up the process by bending the knees before they push down into the ground before springing off the mark. Ask a colleague to observe your method and compare it with the advice given below.

When starting from a stationary position, if you make a determined effort to grip the floor with the toes you will find that your weight is now predominantly forwards. Make sure that your knees are bent before using your quadriceps (thigh) muscles to press downwards before pushing upwards to propel yourself either forwards or backwards.

When starting from a position at a time when some body motion already exists, for example awaiting your opponent's return shot during the rally, try using a bounce start. This is achieved by first ensuring that your knees are bent and that you are balanced. Next press down, by tensing the thigh muscles, and then take the weight off your feet. Both feet will leave the ground for a very small distance and while you are in the air move them into position of one in

Fig 16   Speed off the mark – the bounce start.

front of the other about shoulder width apart. Finally, in one quick continual movement, push off into the required direction. You should experience a bouncing sensation. Initially, try this method slowly and in stages until you are able to blend the stages together to produce a continual movement from start to finish.

Stopping

The ability to stop correctly after moving to a new position on the badminton court should be practised until it is an automatic and efficient process. Most of the time when moving back down the court or sideways across the court you will do so while facing the net. Periodically, for example, when required to play the backhand overhead shots, you will move towards the rearcourt with your back to the net.

The penalty for not being able to stop effectively after any movement could place you well out of position for the next response from your opponent or, more seriously, result in injury. It will help if you consider this aspect of your play in three separate parts: stopping when moving away from the net, stopping when moving sideways across the court and stopping after moving towards the net.

When moving away from the net or across a badminton court, your prime aim should be to get quickly into position so that you can stop and hit the shuttle as you begin to move towards a new base. Unfortunately, this is not always possible and quite often you will be late getting into the hitting position and be forced to play your shot while on the move. In such circumstances the speed with which you can stop becomes a vital part of your recovery and movement to a new position ready to cope with the next shot.

No matter what method you choose to move away from the net or across the court, the best way to stop remains the same. It is simply a matter of creating a base to give stability while forcing your body weight upwards and towards the direction from which you came. This base is obtained by simply making your last stride larger than the others before it. The degree of success of this action will be limited if your upper body continues to move after the last larger stride has been taken, so every effort should be made to keep the movement of this part of you to a minimum.

To stop effectively when moving forwards can be more difficult as most players travel forwards much more quickly than backwards. The advice here is to take a small preparatory step with the penultimate stride before extending the racket leg forwards to take you into the required hitting position. To overcome the likelihood of further movement forwards after you have hit the shuttle, concentrate on becoming centred quickly by reaching upwards with your head. This action will help you maintain your balance and stability and once again will be more easily achieved if the movement of the upper body is kept to an absolute minimum.

Footwork

Good footwork can provide the player with the following:

● The opportunity to play a greater variety of shots
● The chance to hit the shuttle early while it is still above net height
● The ability to recover quickly and narrow gaps
● The chance to deprive your opponents of time
● Balance
● Confidence

Moving forwards is probably easier than moving backwards or sideways and as a result most players find they are quicker approaching the net than moving away from it. Furthermore, when moving backwards many players have an understandable fear of falling over – and as a result they move back with considerable apprehension. Consequently, if your footwork is good and your balance is maintained, you will not only have the ability to move around the court in all directions with confidence, you will also feel capable of increasing your speed.

USEFUL TIP

Be light on your feet. Try to move around the court quietly.

Footwork Forwards

After your start phase has been completed the quickest method to move forwards is by running. If you are tall or have a long stride, you will only have to take one or two paces before reaching the centre of the midcourt; two more paces would carry you to the forecourt if necessary. Whatever the number of paces required, always travel forwards with good posture and your racket held in the ready position.

When dealing with a shuttle in the forecourt, remember that it is the racket head, needs to make contact and not you! Therefore there is no requirement for you to take your whole body into the forecourt area. You should estimate when to stop so that one final stride will take you forward into the hitting position.

Footwork Backwards

Here you have a choice. Moving backwards away from the net can be achieved effectively by running, skipping or a chassé movement.

Whichever method you choose – and you should take the time to try all three – there are three actions that are common to each. First, before moving back, move the racket shoulder back by twisting your trunk a quarter turn, second keep the feet close to the ground as you move and third make the last stride the largest to help you stop and achieve balance and stability.

Running backwards is achieved by moving the feet in turn behind each other. As you travel backwards keep the upper part of the body and the head as still as possible to maintain good posture and balance.

When skipping backwards, the non-racket leg remains well in front of the other leg at all times and the racket leg kicks backwards to commence each stride.

The chassé movement is similar to skipping but is achieved by bringing the non-racket leg back in line at the side of the racket leg before the latter is then moved backwards to commence the next step.

Footwork Sideways

You are advised to master moving sideways in stages – to the racket side, to the non-racket side and then from one side to the other as a continuous movement.

Stand astride the centre line with your knees slightly bent and your feet shoulder width apart. You are now going to move to your racket side to reach, with your racket, an imaginary shuttle that is in the tramlines. Load the quadriceps muscles by pressing downwards before pushing up and off towards the side of the court. The footwork is a sideways chassé. The sequence is left foot into right before the right foot is taken out sideways away from the

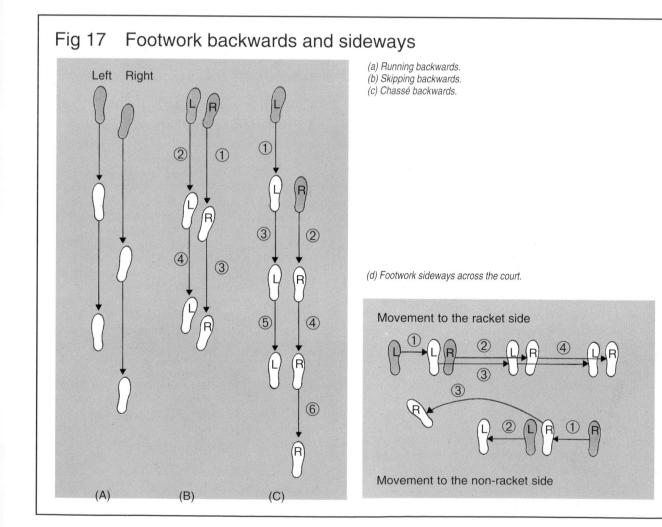

Fig 17   Footwork backwards and sideways

(a) Running backwards.
(b) Skipping backwards.
(c) Chassé backwards.

(d) Footwork sideways across the court.

Movement to the racket side

Movement to the non-racket side

(A)   (B)   (C)

left. The final stride with the racket leg should enable you to reach the tramlines with your outstretched arm and racket. Keep the upper body still and try not to drop the head. Reverse the process to return to the start position.

Movement to the non-racket side requires the same footwork sequence except the opposite foot leads. Your final stride can be taken by either extending the non-racket leg out to the side, or by pivoting on this foot to allow you to swing the racket leg across and in front of you towards the tramlines.

Changing Direction

As you move towards the net there will be occasions when you need to change the direction in which you are travelling from running in a straight line to moving diagonally to a particular corner of the forecourt. Such movements, known as transitions, are easy to apply if you are moving forwards on balance. To change course to the right you use your left leg to provide the power to push off in the new direction, and when altering course to the left the right leg provides the force. As you turn your body towards the new route, keep the head and upper body upright.

The Lunge and Recovery

Although these actions are usually associated with strokes played from the forecourt, you will be required to lunge and recover from all areas of the court. With very few exceptions it is the racket leg that leads in what is no more than an extension to take you into the hitting area.

Figs 18–20 The lunge

The knee of the racket leg is in line with the toe and the non–racket heel is turned inwards to give stability.

Fig 19   Lunge into the right forecourt.

Fig 18   A deep lunge into the forecourt.

Fig 20   Lunge into the left forecourt.

KEY POINT

Never stand with your legs completely straight and rigid. Improve your speed off the mark by keeping your knees flexed.

Before explaining the body skill involved it is worth considering that the wider the lunge the more demanding the recovery. Therefore, if it is possible for you to travel quickly enough to reach the shuttle with a half to lunge, so much the better.

To slow down at the end of your travel phase a smaller stride is taken with the non-racket leg before the lunge is performed. It is important for reasons of balance to turn the heel of the non-racket foot inwards before extending the racket leg out towards the shuttle. As the knee is a hinged joint designed to move forwards and backwards only, the racket leg should be controlled so that the knee is not allowed to travel beyond a vertical line drawn up from the foot or worse still be called upon to bear any weight while twisted out of line.

To promote good posture and balance, and so aid the recovery, keep the upper body and head upright and still. If a full lunge is required to reach a shuttle falling near to the ground, extend the final stride and lower yourself downwards without bending at the waist.

The recovery is achieved by either bringing the racket leg back to the non-racket leg – the preferred method if you intend adopting a forward attacking stance in the forecourt with the feet shoulder width apart – or by taking the non-racket leg towards the racket leg. This latter method, which can become a continuous movement as the lunge is carried out, is useful if you anticipate moving quickly out of the forecourt to cope with a shot played towards the midcourt or rearcourt areas.

Fig 20a Susi Susanti (Indonesia) retrieves with a deep lunge and still retains balance.

CHAPTER 7
THE FOREHAND THROWING ACTION

In most racket sports, when playing shots from above the head, players find their forehand side is far stronger than the backhand. This is especially true in badminton and because a considerable amount of force is required to hit a shuttle that weighs next to nothing a reasonable distance, overhead shots should be played with the forehand action, in preference to the backhand, whenever time permits. Coaches are often heard advising players to 'run around it and take it on the forehand'. It follows therefore that because a far greater number of overhead strokes should be played on the racket side, it is of the utmost importance to learn and master the correct forehand throwing technique.

You would be foolish to assume that during a match sufficient time is available for you to complete a perfect throwing action on every occasion the shuttle comes your way. There will certainly be moments when time is not available and improvisation is required. However, on such occasions, if the basic throwing action has become a natural part of your game, deviations from it will be much easier to achieve.

The key to a successful throwing action is the link between the transfer of body weight and the movement of the shoulders. The technique can be

Figs 21–23 The forehand throwing action viewed from the side

Fig 21   Side view showing the weight on the rear leg.

Fig 22   Moving the racket into the hitting area with the weight now transferred to the front, non–racket leg.

Fig 23   The follow through and start of the recovery movement to a new base.

practised initially off court and without a racket until an acceptable movement has been gained in shadow form. It is advisable to work in pairs or groups to watch and advise each other, but if this is not possible try to carry out your work in front of a mirror.

Stand upright feet about 12in (30cm) apart, shoulders square with an imaginary ball in your racket hand. Keeping the head still and your feet firmly on the ground, twist the trunk at the waist so that the racket shoulder goes well back and the other moves forwards. You should now be looking over the non-racket shoulder.

Make sure that both arms are raised up enough to bring the elbows

KEY POINT

Get your shoulder well back. Imagine you are pulling back an arrow ready for release from a bow.

in line with the shoulders and that the forearms are pointing upwards. Next take a pace forward with the non-racket leg; pause and adjust the position so that your weight is predominantly on the rear (racket) leg. You are now ready to commence the throw. Before doing so focus your mind on what you need to achieve

next: you are going to exchange the positions of the shoulders while walking forwards keeping the body and head upright.

Carry out the next movements slowly making sure that you do them together. Leaving the non-racket leg where it is, push off with the racket leg and take a pace forwards, change the shoulders, straighten the racket arm as it comes forwards and release the ball when the hand is above and just in front of the head. You should finish looking over the racket shoulder, which is now leading. Practise until you can complete the movement at speed with fluency and balance.

Figs 24–26 The forehand throwing action, frontal view

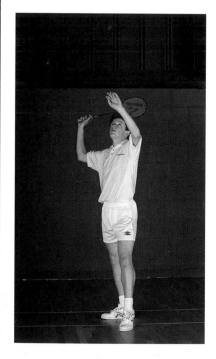 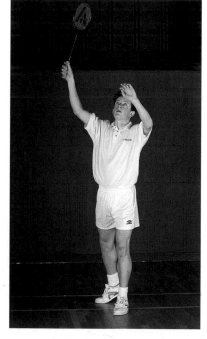 

Fig 24   Racket hand cocked. Non–racket hand assisting balance.

Fig 25   Good posture. Racket shoulder coming forward.

Fig 26   Racket shoulder and leg have now come through.

CHAPTER 8

INDIVIDUAL STROKE PRODUCTION

The aim of this chapter is to deal with the production of each stroke. Before examining the strokes in detail, some discussion of the components that combine to make up an individual stroke is necessary so that the analysis of the finished product, by you or a coach, is simplified.

The Stroke Cycle

This is the collective term applied to the following elements:

- The ready position
- The preparation phase
- The hitting action
- The recovery phase

The Ready Position

How and where you stand on a badminton court depends on many different things. The score, whether you are attacking or defending and the likely reply from your opponent are just three of a number of factors that should contribute to your choice of a suitable position of readiness. Whatever position is chosen from the three stances described below, always keep the racket in the ready position with the hand cocked and the elbow flexed.

The *forward attacking stance* (Fig 27) is adopted in anticipation of your opponent's decision to attack your forecourt area. You will note that the racket leg is well forward and the elbows are raised, bringing the racket head level with the top of the net. You are now ready to move forwards quickly – to dab down a poor quality net shot, for example.

In the *backward attacking stance* (Fig 28) the anticipated response from your opponent is an attempt to lift the shuttle to an area behind you. The adoption of this position of readiness, with the racket leg back, enables you to move quickly to the rear but retains for you a firm base on which to pivot

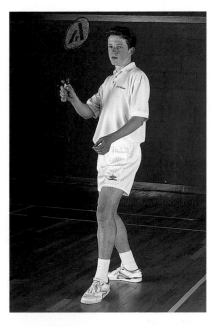

Fig 27   Forward attacking stance. The racket leg is leading, the racket is held ready and the player is prepared to move quickly forwards.

Fig 28   Backward attacking stance. The non–racket leg is leading, the racket is held ready and the player is prepared to move quickly backwards.

Fig 29   Deep defensive stance. Here the player is in a doubles rally anticipating a smash to her non–racket side or the body. Note the flexed knees, firm base and good posture.

and lunge forwards should the need arise. This stance is used extensively as the ready position for the return of the serve.

The *deep defensive stance* (Fig 29) is used when defending and expecting a fierce smash to your midcourt or body. Notice that the shoulders are square to the net, the knees are well flexed, the posture is good and the racket head is just above waist height.

The Preparation Phase

This takes you into the hitting zone and your racket to the start position for the hitting action. This phase may include starting, travelling and stopping, but this depends on the situation, where your opponent has directed the shuttle and what amount of time is available.

The Hitting Action

Here the selection of the correct hitting technique – push, tap or whip – is important and in addition, if the desired shuttle trajectory is to be achieved, you must consider the angle of the racket face and the point of impact at which the racket meets the shuttle.

The Recovery Phase

Once you have despatched the shuttle on its way, the recovery of you and your racket to a new base and suitable stance must be completed as fast as possible to reduce the number of options available to your opponent. This is particularly important when playing singles.

The Strokes

The majority of newcomers to racket sports who are self taught produce strokes automatically without any thought being given to what they are trying to achieve. In badminton, during the early stages of their development, and especially so in the doubles, they remain content, almost relieved, simply to get the shuttle over the net as best they can in the circumstances. Later, through a

Figs 30–32   Dealing with a shot to the right rearcourt

Fig 30   In the ready position in the midcourt.

Fig 31   The preparation phase including travel towards the rearcourt.

Fig 32   In position and producing a forehand overhead clear.

process of trial and error, continual defeat or advice from a partner or coach, the learning process begins.

Before you begin attempting to produce the strokes, look at the overhead and underarm stroke diagrams (Figs 64 to 65) and the headings of the columns in Table 2; from these charts you should be able to gain sufficient information about each stroke, before you start, to enable you to apply yourself to the task with a sense of purpose knowing what you are trying to achieve.

The Point of Impact

The point of impact is the term used to define the position of the shuttle in relation to you when it meets with the face of the racket. You will soon appreciate that it is a vital part of successful stroke production as it helps you to apply a variety of angles on to the flight of the shuttle. You may have immaculate footwork, a superb throwing action and an astute sense of tactics, but all these qualities will be useless if point of impact applied to your stroke is incorrect.

Which Stroke First?

Which stroke to learn first and in what order to tackle the others has been discussed at length by coaches. It would be unwise to set a particular sequence in tablets of stone, but the order shown in Table 2 is recommended as it does lend itself to natural progression and often means that two or more shots can be practised together, providing a useful means of revision. For example, by learning the high serve first you will have hit the shuttle into the air to the rear of the court, the position from which the second shot – the overhead clears – are played.

Serving

In badminton you may gain points only by winning the rally that starts with your serve. Therefore it can be considered to be the most important stroke in the game. Unlike tennis, where the serve can be hit

---

Figs 33–35   The point of impact

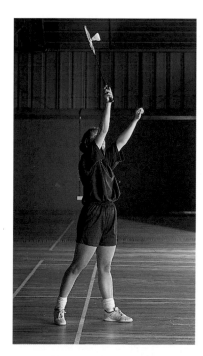

Fig 33   The forehand overhead defensive clear and slow drop shot.

Fig 34   The forehand overhead attacking clear.

Fig 35   The forehand overhead fast drop shot and smash

downwards at speed, the laws of badminton are strictly worded to make sure that at the start of the serve the shuttle must be hit upwards. Such are the restrictions in the lawful execution of this stroke that many coaches believe that at the start of the rally it is the receiver who is best placed to gain an early advantage.

USEFUL TIP

On winning the toss you can elect to serve, not to serve, or choose ends. If you do win the toss it is wise to serve. If you do not you may never have the chance to score a point.

For these reasons alone the serve requires considerable practice so that it can be delivered accurately and consistently. Your serve will seldom become an outright winner, but a well executed serve may produce a response that provides you with the early initiative in the opening part of the rally. There are four types of serve:

- The low serve
- The high serve
- The flick serve
- The drive serve

It is possible to play all four with a forehand or backhand action. However, because your forehand strokes are usually the stronger of the two, the high serve is rarely produced successfully with a backhand action.

Each of the four serves is delivered differently; they have their own flight pattern and vary in speed. Consequently, you will need to decide which of the serves to play. Your choice can be influenced by many things, including the score, the receiver's position and whether you are playing singles or doubles. This section of the book deals only with the technical production of each serve; the tactical considerations and the subsequent choice of serve are covered in Part 3.

KEY POINT

Plan your serve. Consider the position of your opponent and what the likely return could be before you hit the shuttle.

The Backhand Low Serve

This is the easiest serve to produce if you keep your movements to a minimum. In fact, if you can limit the moving parts to the racket arm only during the hitting phase, so much the better. The aim is to serve so that the shuttle passes over the net as low as possible and for it to land on or just inside the front service line of the opposing service court.

There are numerous schools of thought regarding the position of the feet in the preliminary stance to be adopted. If there is one method more common than others to be seen in use by the better players it is with the racket foot leading. However, this does not mean that you have to follow suit. Whether you lead with the racket or non-racket foot, or stand with your feet astride in line with each other, is a personal matter for you to explore. In choosing what is best for you, consider that you need to face the net, stand still on a firm base to begin with, then have the ability to move quickly off your base once the shuttle has been struck.

A firm base is achieved by placing the feet about shoulder width apart with the knees slightly bent. Bend forwards very slightly from the waist and make sure that your weight is on the balls of the feet. Keep the shuttle behind you at this stage in your non-racket hand. Hold your racket in a backhand grip well out in front of you so that the strings are facing the net. You should make sure that the whole of the head of the racket is clearly below all parts of your racket hand. It is important to achieve a gap of about 18in (45cm) between the racket and your body at the start, so that you can achieve a smooth arm movement when commencing the hitting phase. With the shuttle held (base down) by the skirt or feathers in the fingers of the non-racket hand, bring it from behind you to a position directly in front of the racket face but no higher than the waist. The racket will be far enough away from you if the non-racket arm is now perfectly straight. You are now ready to commence the hitting phase of your backhand low serve.

Keeping everything else still, and in particular the non-racket arm straight, take the whole of the racket arm back into the body, bending the arm at the elbow; pause and then start what is your first forward movement with the racket since the shuttle was placed in front of it.

The hitting technique required is a push, and so long as your forward arm movement is not hurried and you do not flick the racket hand, you should be able to push the shuttle low over the net and into the opposing service court. Under no circumstances should you hit the shuttle from above your waist! On completion, bring the elbows up and the racket into the ready position.

The Forehand Low Serve

Compared to the backhand low serve, there is a lot more movement required in the production of this stroke. Therefore, it is not as easy to produce successfully and considerable care should be taken.

Stand with your feet shoulder width apart with the non-racket foot leading and pointing to the centre of the net. Put your weight on to the rear (racket) leg, pointing your toes towards the

Figs 36–38 The backhand low serve

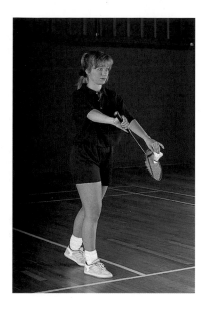

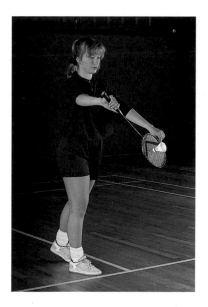

Fig 36   In position. Note the firm base, the straight non–racket arm and the position of the shuttle well away from the body.

Fig 37   Preparing to hit the shuttle. Only the racket arm has moved (back).

Fig 38   The point of impact with the shuttle still well out to the front.

Figs 39–41 The forehand low serve

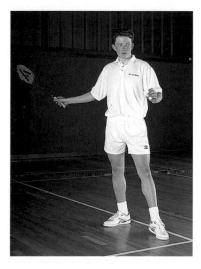

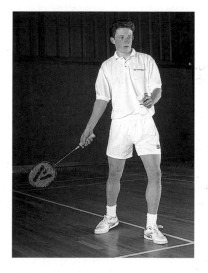

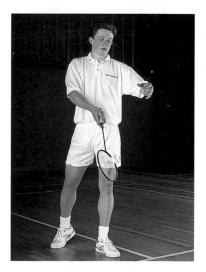

Fig 39   In position. The feet are shoulder width apart, weight is on the racket leg, the racket arm is well back and the hand is cocked at the wrist.

Fig 40   The serve has commenced. The arm is swinging downwards, the weight moving on to the non–racket leg while retaining good balance and posture.

Fig 41   The point of impact. Note that the racket hand has remained cocked.

net post that is on your racket side. Make sure that this stance is comfortable and make minor adjustments if it is not, because you are going to transfer the weight from the rear leg to the front leg as you commence the hitting action and you need to retain your balance. Hold the shuttle well out in front of you by the forefinger and thumb of the non-racket hand with the base pointing straight down towards the floor.

With your racket held in a forehand grip, cock the hand back, flex the elbow and take the racket back behind you until the forearm is parallel to the floor and the back of the racket hand is facing the ceiling. The head of the racket should now be pointing in an upwards direction. You are now ready to commence the hitting action of the serve.

Bearing in mind that the first forward movement of your racket signifies the start of the serve, focus your mind on achieving a flight path that takes the shuttle as low as possible over the net. Ideally, the shuttle should reach its highest point as it passes close to the top of the net. Immediately it has passed over it should then begin to drop so that it lands on or just inside the front service line of the opposite court. The hitting technique used is a push, and this can be achieved by swinging the racket arm downwards, forwards and upwards slowly (like a pendulum on a clock) while transferring your weight on to the non-racket leg.

It is important to keep your racket hand cocked back during the swing and that the swing itself is continuous. As the racket passes forward of the

non-racket leg and starts to move upwards, allow the shuttle to drop on to the centre of your racket face. The momentum of the arm swing should enable you to push the shuttle delicately on its way low over the net. Once you have struck the shuttle, bring your elbows up and the racket into the ready position.

The High Serve

The aim of this serve is to move your opponent into the rear of his service court area. There is no requirement to make any attempt to deceive your opponent while performing the serve. The shuttle should be hit high into the air so that it falls downwards steeply and as far back as possible into the opposite service court.

Figs 42–44   The high serve

Fig 42   In position. Weight is on the racket leg, the racket is well back and the hand is cocked at the wrist.

Fig 43   The point of impact with the weight now on the non–racket leg.

Fig 44   Frontal view showing the end of the follow through of this whip–action stroke. Note the position of the racket arm over the non–racket shoulder.

Your initial stance and the way you hold the shuttle in a position well out in front of you should be identical to that used for the forehand low serve. The transfer of weight from the rear racket leg to the front non-racket leg during the hitting phase should also be the same. However, as the hitting technique applied is a whip action, the arm swing must be carried out at speed so that sufficient power can be created to achieve plenty of height and depth on the shuttle.

The direction of the shuttle will be determined by the angle of the racket face on contact with the shuttle and the early part of the follow through thereafter. Therefore, it is very important to hit the shuttle with a flat racket face otherwise a sliced serve that lands out of court could occur! Remember to straighten the hand on impact and then carry out your follow through in two stages. First, follow through for about 18in (45cm) with your racket aimed in the direction that you wish the shuttle to go. Then, second, allow your racket arm to complete the swing over the non-racket shoulder. On completion of the follow through, bring your racket down into the ready position.

The Flick Serve

Even though you may have practised your low serve regularly and developed a stroke that is both accurate and consistent, there will be numerous occasions when you fail to gain an early initiative. This is because your opponent anticipates or gambles and moves quickly forwards, reaches the shuttle early and is able to play a return of serve that puts you under immediate pressure. Such moves feature prominently in the doubles game and to counter them you should develop the ability to vary your serve with disguised alternatives. One such method is the flick serve. The aim is to produce, with a low serve action, a serve of medium height that sends the shuttle behind

your opponent and to the rear of his service court.

The disguise should be such that your opponent commits himself to coping with what he believes will be a low serve to the front of the court. You should strive hard not to telegraph your intentions in any way – by racket movement, body language, facial expression or a communication to your partner that is overheard. The hitting technique, a tap action, should be applied following a slow arm swing identical to that used for the low serve.

Both the back and forehand serve actions can be adapted to produce flick serves, but tactical considerations need to be addressed, as outlined in Part 3. The following paragraphs deal only with the actions required to produce the stroke.

You will recall keeping your racket hand cocked back during the forehand swing used in the forehand low serve. The forehand flick is achieved by straightening the racket hand at the last moment; this not only generates a faster speed on the racket head but alters the angle of the racket face at the point of impact with the shuttle. It is these two adjustments that achieve the increased shuttle speed and greater height that are essential to the success of this serve.

For the backhand low serve you did not need to cock the hand back. Consequently, the requirement to increase the speed and height on the shuttle by generating a faster speed on the racket head is more difficult. For this reason some players, unwisely, choose not to cultivate a backhand low serve because they feel it limits them to low serves only and, more importantly, provides the more astute receiver with the knowledge that he will never have to deal with anything but them!

The production of a successful backhand flick serve is more difficult for those players who, mindful of the law that insists that the racket head is

clearly below the racket hand, choose to produce the backhand low serve with the shaft of the racket held perpendicularly. Whatever method you have adopted for your backhand low serve, to produce a flick action without having your hand cocked back initially calls for assistance from elsewhere and it is the racket thumb that should be utilized.

At the last moment, when your racket wrist is about 6in (15cm) behind the shuttle, and the racket face is pointing towards the desired direction, press hard with your thumb on to the racket handle (as if ringing a door bell in a temper) and flick the racket head forwards as fast as you can. Once the flick serve is delivered, quickly bring the racket back into the ready position ready for your opponent's return.

The Drive Serve

The aim of the drive serve is to hit a fast and flat shuttle that will exploit a weakness in your opponent's technique or produce a response for which you have made adequate provision. It is a difficult stroke to disguise and because the shuttle continues to rise after it has crossed the net into your opponent's service court, unless it meets with continued success it is best used infrequently.

It can be produced with both the back and forehand serving actions. To achieve as flat a trajectory as possible, make sure the shuttle is only just below the waist at the point of impact. The action should be identical to that used for your backhand and forehand low serves until the last moment when you should speed up the racket arm quickly and punch at the shuttle.

Be careful not to use the wrist as this will cause the shuttle to rise more sharply with disastrous results: this serve could, if left by the receiver, go out of court at the back service line. Therefore careful judgement of power is required so that a crisp shot is achieved with the racket head kept down below your hand. As always, on completion of the serve bring your racket quickly to the normal ready position or a spot adjusted to help you cope with the likely reply.

Foul Serves

As you gain experience in badminton you will come to appreciate the importance of the serve. This is especially so in doubles where you will undoubtedly find the quality of your serve being put to test by an aggressive receiver. In your efforts to develop a serve that skims the net, be careful not to produce a foul serve.

THE SERVE – LAWS CHECK

- Some part of both feet of the server and receiver must remain in contact with the surface of the court in a stationary position until the serve is delivered.

- The server's racket must hit the base of the shuttle while the whole of the shuttle is below the waist.

- At the instant of hitting the shuttle when serving the whole of the head of the racket must be discernibly below the whole of the hand holding the racket.

- The first forward movement of the server's racket head is the start of the serve.

- The movement of the server's racket must continue forwards after the start of the serve.

Forehand Overhead Shots

It is assumed that the forehand throwing action, covered in Chapter 7,

Fig 45   An example of an illegal forehand service – the whole of the head of the racket is not discernibly below the whole of the hand holding the racket.

Fig 46   An example of an illegal backhand service – the server's racket is hitting the base of the shuttle while the shuttle is above the waist.

has been understood because this movement is fundamental to the successful production of shots that are the most common in the game: the forehand overhead family.

The Defensive Overhead Clear

The prime aim of this stroke is to make time for yourself so that recovery into position can take place before the shuttle enters your opponent's hitting zone. Therefore plenty of height on the shuttle is required and this is best achieved by a whip action with the point of impact above the racket shoulder. Always try to strike the shuttle as you move forwards.

The Attacking Overhead Clear

Although the shuttle is hit upwards on what appears to be a defensive pathway, this stroke when played with accuracy is a useful attacking measure. The shuttle is hit with a whip action and is sent at speed to the rearcourt. By bringing the point of impact forwards, a lower trajectory is achieved, which deprives your opponents of time.

The Slow Drop Shot

If this shot is to be successful, the shuttle must land in the forecourt as close to the net as possible. The point of impact is above the racket shoulder; the push action that is

Figs 47–48   The forehand defensive overhead clear

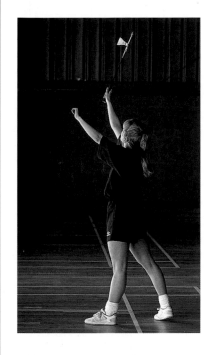 

Fig 47   Viewed from the non–racket side. Note the point of impact.

Fig 48   Frontal view showing the flat racket face.

required is introduced at the last possible moment and adds an element of deception. Normally used as a creative shot, the intention is to bring your opponent late into the forecourt – from where you hope he will produce a weak underarm response that is hit into the air only part way into your midcourt.

The Fast Drop Shot

This shot attacks the front of your opponent's midcourt area and is best directed to the sides. While the throwing action remains the same as the slow version, the hitting action and point of impact are changed to produce a shuttle that travels on a more shallow trajectory at a faster speed. The tap action is used and the point of impact is in front of you. This stroke, which if successful forces your opponent to take the shuttle close to the ground, is especially useful in mixed doubles as it entices both players to move to the side of the court to attempt a reply.

The Smash

As the name implies, this stroke is a power stroke played with an aggressive whip action as a clear attempt to finish off the rally. A steep trajectory, achieved by bringing the point of impact to the front of you, is required. Unless you play this shot at the right time, on balance and with the ability to recover quickly, your opponent's response can quickly gain him the initiative. It is especially important to appreciate that as you move away from the forecourt your smash will become flatter and less powerful.

Forehand Underarm Shots

The Underarm Clear

Often referred to as the lob, this stroke is usually played from your forecourt area into your opponent's rearcourt. Like the overhead clear, the flight pattern can be varied to gain time for yourself or deprive your opponent of it. The hitting action, a tap or a whip, is usually dependent on the situation in which you find yourself.

If you are late to the shuttle, short of time and taking it low down, a whip action is required to gain height on the shuttle while you recover. By comparison, if you are early to the shuttle, have plenty of time and are able to make contact with the shuttle at about chest height, the use of a tap action will suffice. In addition, in these circumstances, it would be easy to add a deceptive element to your play because a push net return to your opponent's forecourt becomes another option available to you.

The point of impact should be well out in front of you with the racket leg leading in the lunge position. Always keep your head up and avoid bending the upper body from the waist.

The Forehand Net Shot

All shots that require a push action need to be played with care because there is less room for error. Such is the case with this stroke. This shot is played when the shuttle has gone over the net and is falling downwards. Always try to play it early; never allow

Fig 49   A forehand net shot with the shuttle taken early at the top of the net.

Backhand Overhead Shots

The Overhead Clear

Players consider that this stroke is the most technically difficult to master and the fact that the complete backhand overhead clear action is not such a natural movement as the forehand equivalent is indisputable. The main cause of the weakness is obvious yet seldom addressed – players do not practise it as much as their forehand strokes!

Any uncontrolled knock up between two players usually starts with an underarm lift and is then followed by an exchange of forehand overhead strokes thereafter. To make matters worse, players are coached to improvise with round-the-head forehand shots when faced with the need to play a backhand overhead shot. Therefore, it is little wonder that at club level the number of players with a proficient backhand overhead clear is at a minimum.

The successful production of this stroke should be tackled in stages. First, ignore footwork and concentrate on achieving a clearly identifiable tap action. This can be practised on your own. Hit the shuttle high into the air and as the shuttle falls towards you adopt a backhand grip. Just before you make contact with the shuttle roll the forearm quickly outwards (supination) and flick or tap the shuttle back upwards. Initially this may be difficult but persevere and you will soon achieve the timing necessary to produce a crisp sound as the shuttle is sent high up into the air.

Second, stand in the midcourt facing the net and commence a simple backhand drive rally down the tramlines to a partner positioned directly opposite on the other side of the net. Tap the shuttle slowly to each other so that you can concentrate on the correct adoption of a backhand grip and definite tap action. As the

the shuttle to drop any more than is necessary. Do not take your whole body too close to the shuttle, just remember to lunge correctly to maintain balance and assist recovery. As you go through the preparation phase keep your elbows up and away from your body.

If you can get into the habit of keeping the racket wrist above the head of the racket during the hitting phase, not only will you enjoy better control, you should also be able to deceive your opponents with a deceptive shallow flick over his head as he approaches the forecourt. If you are very close to the net there is no requirement for you to move your racket head upwards to hit the shuttle. It is simply a matter of offering the racket to the shuttle and letting the shuttle bounce off the racket face, which is now held in an outstretched hand, the arm almost straight.

However, there is a need to control the angle of the racket face as this will effect how far away from the net the

shuttle falls into your opponent's forecourt. By turning your racket hand clockwise until the back of the hand faces downwards, you will bring your racket face parallel to the floor and produce quality net returns that fall close to the net on your opponent's side.

The Hairpin Net Shot

This stroke is so named because the flight of the shuttle depicts an inverted hairpin. As the shuttle is struck when it has fallen close to the ground, usually in your forecourt, it is a difficult shot to play with accuracy. Good posture, balance and recovery are crucial if it is to meet with success. The preparation phase will take you into the lunge position and from here it is a matter of squatting down while keeping the head up and the back as straight as possible. The hitting action is a push and your aim is to get the shuttle to climb up and over the net and stay as low as possible.

Figs 50–52 Backhand overhead shots

Fig 50   In position under the shuttle. Note the position of the racket head and the raised elbow.

Fig 51   The point of impact.

Fig 52   Recovering back to a new base.

Fig 53   The ready position.

Fig 54   Player has pivoted on the non–racket leg and turned to move towards the shuttle.

Fig 55   In position ready to start the hitting action.

Fig 56   The point of impact.

rally progresses, try to exaggerate the tap action by turning the base of the racket handle towards the net as the shuttle comes towards you. Now instruct your partner to begin directing the shuttles higher and deeper down the court so that this forces you to begin turning your back to the net as you step across and back with the racket leg to reach the shuttle.

You should now concentrate on the hitting phase: still employing a tap action, point the elbow momentarily at the shuttle as it comes to a position above your head and slightly out to your racket side. The racket leg should be nearest the baseline with the knees slightly flexed. You are now going to straighten your legs and move the racket head at speed up to the shuttle, by the shortest possible route, as you supinate the forearm. Imagine you are using a towel to flick a fly off the bathroom ceiling so that a good tap rebound action is produced with the racket head. Your point of contact should be the same as that of a left-hander who is executing a forehand overhead clear. After you have made contact with the shuttle, twist back in the same direction so that you face the net ready for movement to a new position.

The Overhead Drop Shot

The production of a backhand overhead slow drop shot to the forecourt requires minor adjustment from the clear. Quite simply, instead of using a tap hitting action, the push should be used. No alteration to the point of impact is required but be careful not to make your intentions known with poor body skill and a slow build up during the preparation phase.

Similarly, the backhand fast drop shot to the midcourt is achieved with a tap action. Bring the point of impact forward to achieve a steep trajectory.

Backhand Underarm Shots

The Underarm Clear

Most players find this stroke easier to produce than its forehand counterpart. The same considerations made for the forehand underarm clear apply but two points merit some reinforcement. Unless the correct racket grip is adopted accuracy will become erratic and deception more difficult. Remember to step into the shot with your racket foot and to keep sufficient distance between you and the shuttle. The point of impact should be as high as possible.

The Backhand Net Shot

You will probably find that this stroke is easier to carry out than the forehand equivalent and the end product will be of a better quality. Many coaches believe that this is because the racket arm does not need to be turned as the head of the racket is presented to meet the shuttle and it is therefore easier to perform.

All observations made for the forehand net shot should again be applied and it is especially important that the correct backhand grip is adopted so that an underarm clear can become an easily achieved option. Remember also that the racket leg leads and that good posture and firm balance are paramount.

The Hairpin Net Shot

Similar considerations to those made for the forehand equivalent apply. The racket leg again leads and because this leg is taken across the body

> **USEFUL TIP**
>
> Whatever the hopelessness of the situation, always try to return the shuttle; your opponent may well make an error.

Fig 57   The backhand net shot. Racket leg leads.

towards your non-racket side, balance may be more difficult to achieve as there will be a tendency to drop the head and shoulders.

Other Shots

The Return of the Smash

If you can become proficient in returning your opponent's smashes you will have won two major psychological battles – the first with your opponent and the second with yourself. During the early learning stages of the game far too many players become fearful of coping with smashes. You can employ the push, tap or whip hitting actions when dealing with a smash. Which action is suitable depends on the tactical

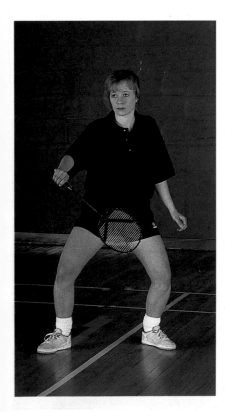

Fig 58   The defensive stance for the backhand push return.

situation you or your team are in and the area to which you intend returning the shuttle.

Remind yourself of the three stances covered earlier within this chapter and note particularly the position of the racket head in each. Occasions will arise when you will be required to return the smash from all three stances.

To build your confidence we will deal first with the most common situation that arises – the requirement to return a smash to your midcourt from an opponent who is positioned in his midcourt area, before covering the other eventualities.

The Backhand Block to the Forecourt

A deep defensive stance with the racket at waist height will enable you to act as a shock absorber. By adopting a backhand grip you will be able to block any smashes directed to the whole of the blue area in Fig 59. Make sure that there is plenty of distance between yourself and the racket and remember not to bend at the waist. As the shuttle comes towards you, present the racket face, move the racket forwards away from you slightly and allow the shuttle to bounce off the strings. To control the speed of the shuttle and how far it travels into the opposite court, alter the angle of the racket face.

The Backhand Push to the Midcourt

Because the intention here is to direct the shuttle beyond the forecourt and into the midcourt, the forward movement of the racket is more pronounced and the angle of the racket face is set almost parallel to the net. The shuttle should travel in a shallow arc, past any forecourt doubles player, into the midcourt.

With your confidence of dealing with this return increasing, additional returns of a more difficult technical

nature can be added to your range of shots.

The Forehand Block and Push Returns to the Forecourt and Midcourt

Using the same stance, you now need to cope with smashes directed to your racket side, the yellow area in Fig 59. All the principles of the backhand returns apply except for the obvious need to adopt a forehand grip. To improve control on the shuttle and to help maintain good posture, bring the elbow of the racket arm into the waist as you make contact with the shuttle.

Returns to the Rearcourt

To be successful in responding to a smash with a return to your opponent's rearcourt, good timing will be required to achieve sufficient height and distance on the shuttle. The return can be played with either a forehand or backhand action – the latter being the more common of the two for cross-court returns in doubles.

For the best results adopt a forward attacking stance and move forward into the shot as contact is made with the shuttle. The point of impact must be well forward and as high as possible; a well timed and firm tap action is needed. Variation in the height of the shuttle will be achieved by changing the angle of the racket face.

Crouched Defence

When successful, this return of the smash is a soul-destroying tool that will do wonders for your confidence. It is played from the front edge of the midcourt as a reply to flat smashes or those played from the rear of the court. It is particularly suitable for the woman player in mixed doubles.

Adopt the forward attacking stance and squat down as necessary so that the racket head is above your hand

Fig 61   This woman is in a crouch defence position waiting to meet the smash

Fig 59   Shuttles directed at the blue area can be considered as backhand returns of the smash, and at the yellow area can be considered as forehand returns of the smash.

Fig 60   Example of a shortened grip for forehand block returns of the smash. Note the position of the elbow close to the waist.

and in line with top of the net. Watch the incoming shuttle carefully and respond with a dab action that will despatch the shuttle quickly back into your opponents' midcourt.

The Forehand Net Kill

The opportunity to play a net kill (often called a dab) usually presents itself following your opponent's loose return to your smash or his poorly executed net shot. What you must remember is that you are going to commit yourself fully to a position close to the net so that you can produce a winner. Failure to do so may well leave you stranded as the shuttle is returned over your head. In addition if any part of you or your racket touches the net it is a fault. For both the forehand and backhand kills, make sure that the point of contact with the shuttle is well forward with the racket face tilted downwards.

During the preparation phase for the forehand net kill, which will

LAWS CHECK

Providing that you make contact with the shuttle on your side of the net, it is not a fault if you follow through with your racket over the net into your opponent's court.

include your travel forwards into the forecourt, keep your elbows up and the racket hand cocked. Your final stride into the hitting area will be with the racket leg. Move your hand halfway up the racket handle and adopt a pan handle grip, which will restrict excessive forward movement of the racket head. Now concentrate on meeting the shuttle at the same time as your racket foot makes final contact with the floor. Using as much controlled force as possible, straighten the hand, dab the shuttle down and recover the racket immediately. To assist your recovery keep the upper body and head upright throughout the stroke and adopt a centred balanced posture as soon as possible after making contact.

The Backhand Net Kill

The preparation for this shot is the same as that used for the forehand kill with the obvious exception that a backhand grip needs to be used. Because the shot involves taking the racket arm across the body on to the non-racket side, some players forget to cock the hand and find it difficult to hit the shuttle with any force. To overcome this raise the racket elbow so that it is in line with the top of the net, and point the end of the racket handle towards the shuttle. Delay your hitting action to the last possible moment by adopting the 'tent peg' principle: imagine that the top end of your racket frame is tied down to a peg positioned in the ground behind you, restricting any forward movement of the racket. At the last possible moment the string is cut allowing you to straighten the hand and bring the racket head through at speed. You should now achieve a much more powerful dab shot that has every chance of being an outright winner.

The Forehand Drive

Drive shots are usually played from the sides of the court when the shuttle has fallen too low for it to be returned with a smash. Usually they are played with pace, but it is possible and often tactically sound to play a drive that falls slowly into the opposing forecourt or midcourt areas. The shuttle should travel horizontally and skim over the net as low as possible. Footwork sideways is used to carry you towards the hitting zone where the racket leg is outstretched for the last stride and the racket arm is then brought around parallel to the ground.

Try to make the point of impact slightly in front of you and to control the angle of the racket face or accuracy will be lost. For shuttles that you wish to direct straight down the tramlines, a tap action should be used so that the racket face stops on impact parallel to the net. For cross-court direction, a whip action used in conjunction with a point of impact slightly nearer the net will send the shuttle inwards from the tramline area.

The Backhand Drive

Whereas the racket leg finishes nearer the tramlines for the forehand drive, either can be used to step into position for the backhand drive. For drives played well to the front of you it is acceptable to step to the side with the non-racket leg. For drives met at the side you should pivot on the non-racket foot and take the racket leg across the body. Cross-court drives require a strong whip action and a pronounced turn of the shoulders so that you contribute body weight into the shot and finish the stroke standing square to the net.

Fig 62   Moving across towards the side tramlines to play a forehand drive.

Fig 63   The point of impact with the racket arm parallel to the ground.

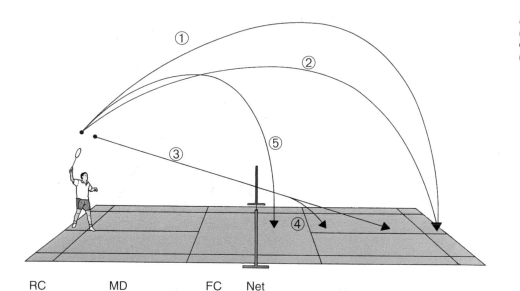

RC   MD   FC   Net

Fig 64   Overhead strokes. Key:
(1) defensive clear, (2) attacking
clear, (3) smash, (4) fast drop shot,
(5) slow drop shot.

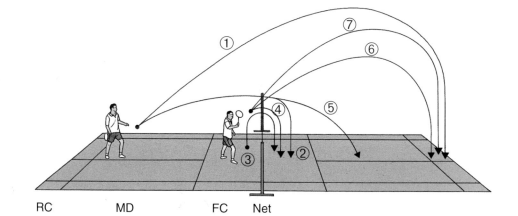

RC   MD   FC   Net

Fig 65   Underarm strokes. Key:
(1) return of smash to rearcourt,
(2) return of smash to forecourt,
(3) hairpin net shot, (4) basic net
shot, (5) return of smash to
midcourt, (6) attacking clear,
(7) defensive clear.

Shot or stroke	Type of shot	Played from	Played to	Hitting technique	Point of impact	Use	Most common in
High serve	Creative shot	Front of midcourt	Rear of midcourt or rearcourt	Whip	Well out to front of non-racket leg	Defence	Singles
Defensive overhead clear	'Hit and hope'	Rear of midcourt or rearcourt	Rearcourt	Whip	Above racket shoulder	Defence	Singles
Attacking overhead clear	Attempted winner or creative shot	Rear of midcourt or rearcourt	Rearcourt	Whip or tap	Above and just in front of racket shoulder	Attack	All games
Slow drop	Creative shot or attempted winner	Rear of midcourt or rearcourt	Forecourt	Push	Above racket shoulder	Attack	Singles and level doubles
Fast drop	Creative shot or attempted winner	Rear of midcourt or rearcourt	Midcourt	Tap	Above and in front of racket shoulder	Attack	Singles and mixed doubles
Smash	Attempted winner	Midcourt or rearcourt	Midcourt	Whip	Above and in front of racket shoulder	Attack	All games
Return of smash	Creative shot, attempted winner or 'hit and hope'	All areas	Midcourt	Push or tap	Well out to front as high as possible	Attack	All games
Net kill	Attempted winner	Forecourt	Midcourt	Tap	Well out to front high as possible	Attack	All games
Net shot	Creative shot	Forecourt	Forecourt	Push	Well out to front high as possible	Attack	All games
Underarm clear	Creative shot or 'hit and hope'	Forecourt or midcourt	Rearcourt	Tap or whip	Well out to front high as possible	Defence	All games
Low serve	Creative shot	Front of midcourt	Front of midcourt	Push	Well out in front of non-racket leg	Attack	Doubles
Flick serve	Creative shot or attempted winner	Front of midcourt	Rear of midcourt	Tap	Well out in front of non-racket leg	Attack	Doubles
Drive serve	Creative shot or attempted winner	Front of midcourt	Midcourt	Push	Well out in front of non-racket leg	Attack	Doubles
Drives	Creative shot or attempted winner	Side of midcourt	All areas	Tap or whip	Shoulder height	Attack	Doubles

Table 2   Stroke table.

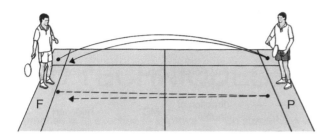

Practice 5 – Grip Changes (on court)

The player stands in the tramlines in the ready position; the feeder stands opposite. They play a continuous underarm rally.

Conditions:
The racket head is below the hand. The feeder can direct shots to either side of the player. Play three sets.

Coaching points:
The hitting action is a push. The player should bring the racket back to the central ready position after each shot. If a pace forward is required, the racket foot leads.

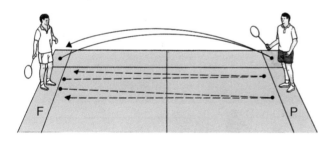

Practice 6 – The Tap

The player stands in the midcourt, facing the net in the ready position. The feeder stands in opposite midcourt. They play a continuous rally, keeping the racket head above the hand.

Conditions:
Play four sets. In the first set the feeder feeds to the forehand side of the player. In the second set the feeder feeds to the backhand side. In the third set the feeder feeds to alternate sides. In the fourth set the feeder feeds to either side. The feeder and the player play a flat rally, skimming the net.

Coaching points:
The hitting action is a tap. The elbows should be kept up and the racket head should return to the centre quickly after each tap. Players should flex their knees to squat down as required, and avoid bending at the waist.

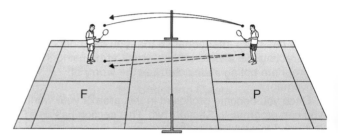

Practice 7 – The Push

The player stands in the forecourt in the forward attacking stance. The feeder stands in the midcourt. They play a continuous rally with the racket head above the hand.

Conditions:
Play four sets. In the first set the feeder feeds to the forehand; in the second set to the backhand; in the third set to alternate sides; in the fourth set to either side. The player should aim for the feeder's waist.

Coaching points:
The hitting action is a push. The racket head should return to the centre quickly after each push. The players flex their knees to squat down as required.

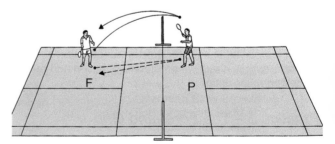

Practice 8 – The Tap and Push

The player stands in the forecourt. The feeder stands in the rear of the midcourt. They play a continuous rally with the racket head above the hand.

Conditions:
Play two sets. The feeder feeds to either side of the player. In the first set the player plays alternate taps and pushes. In the second set the feeder calls out to nominate a tap or push shot for the player's return.

Coaching points:
The hitting action is a tap or push. The elbows should be kept up, and variation in the shuttle speed should be seen.

Coaching points:
The hitting action is a whip. The player should adopt an open shoulder stance and follow through over his non-racket shoulder.

Practice 10 – The Forehand Overhead Clear

The player stands in the rearcourt. The feeder stands in the front of the midcourt. The feeder hits high serves and the player returns forehand overhead clears to the opposite rearcourt.

Conditions:
Play two sets. In the first set play defensive clears; in the second set play attacking clears.

Coaching points:
The hitting action is a whip. The player must adjust the point of impact and all clears should land in the rearcourt. The feeder should observe height and assess outcome.

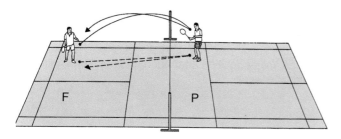

Practice 9 – The High Serve for Singles

The player stands in the front of the midcourt. The feeder observes in the opposite rearcourt. The player plays high serves to the rearcourt.

Conditions:
Play two sets. The laws of service apply. In the first set the player serves from the right midcourt to the right rearcourt. In the second set he serves from the left midcourt to the left rearcourt.

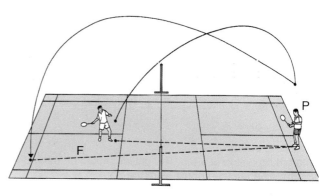

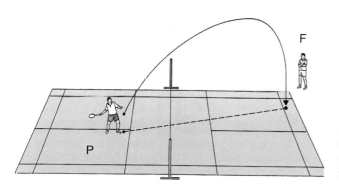

Practice 11 – The Forehand Overhead Slow Drop Shot

The player stands in the rearcourt. The feeder stands in the front of the midcourt. The feeder hits high serves to the player, who returns slow drop shots to the opposite forecourt.

Conditions:
Play two sets. The shuttle should land in the forecourt.

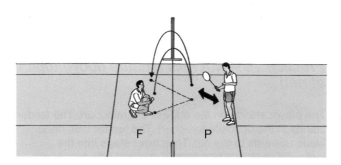

Practice 18 – Underarm Clears

The player stands on the 'T' and the feeder stands in the opposite forecourt. The feeder hand feeds shuttles into the player's forecourt. The player lunges and returns shuttles to the rearcourt.

Conditions:
Play three sets. In the first set the feeder feeds to the player's forehand side. In the second set the feeder feeds to the player's backhand side. In the third set the feeder feeds to either side. The player should recover fully between shots.

Coaching points:
The hitting action is a tap. The player should lunge correctly with the racket leg leading and should keep his head up.

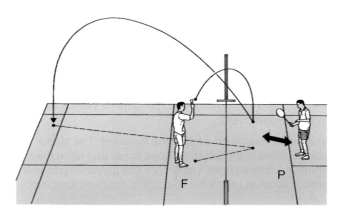

Practice 19 – The Low Serves

The player stands in the front of the midcourt. The feeder observes while the player serves to the target areas.

Conditions:
Play two sets. The laws of service apply. In the first set the player should hit forehand serves. In the second set he should hit backhand serves.

Coaching points:
The hitting action is a push and the shuttle should skim the net. The player must adopt the ready position on completion.

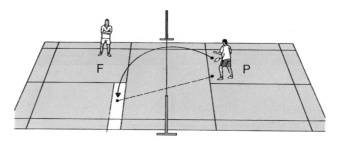

Practice 20 – The Flick Serve

The player stands in the front of the midcourt, while the feeder observes. The player flick serves to the target areas.

Conditions:
Play one set. The laws of service apply. The serve and flick serve should alternate and the shuttle must reach the rear of the midcourt.

Coaching points:
The hitting action, a tap, is used at the last possible moment.

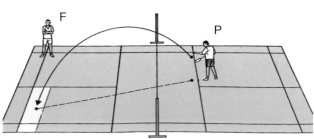

Practice 21 – The Drive Serve

The player stands in the front of the midcourt. The feeder observes and the player hits drive serves to the target areas.

Conditions:
Play one set. The laws of service apply.

Coaching points:
The hitting action is a push, the arm swing fast. The shuttle trajectory should be shallow, with the hand cocked back throughout.

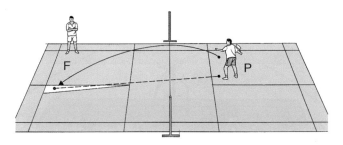

Practice 22 – The Drives

The player stands in the midcourt. The feeder stands close to the net in the forecourt and hand feeds shuttles to the tramlines. The player lunges sideways to return the shuttle to the forecourt, midcourt or rearcourt.

Conditions:
Play three sets. In the first set the feeds should be to the player's forehand; in the second set to the player's backhand. In the third set the player should hit cross-court drives (the feeder should duck down after each feed).

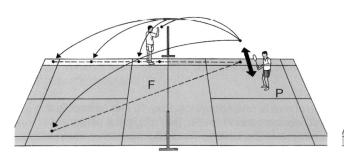

Coaching points:
The hitting action is taps in the first and second set, whips in the third. The arm should come around parallel to the ground. The shuttle should skim the net.

Practice Routines – Section Two

The practices that follow are designed to exercise a player in all elements of the stroke cycle. Some of the practices involve more than one stroke and when carried out properly create a simulated game.

The practices in this section are more physically demanding than those contained within Section One and their success depends on the quality of the player's strokes and movement. Strokes and tactics are inseparable; poor strokes will have an adverse effect on tactics. If you find that a particular stroke or movement is poor and that this prevents you completing the practice satisfactorily, return to Section One or to Chapters 5, 6 and 8 and revise as necessary.

Practice 23 – Movement Backwards and Forwards and the Forehand Overhead Clear

The player stands in the midcourt. The feeder stands in the front of the midcourt. The feeder hits high serves to the rearcourt. The player moves back to the rearcourt, hits a forehand overhead clear to the opposite rearcourt and returns to the midcourt.

Conditions:
Play one set. The player should hit high defensive clears.

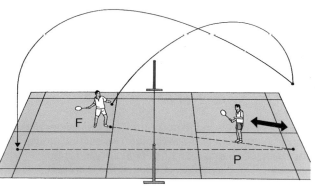

Coaching points:
The hitting action is a push. The players should maintain their balance throughout. They play a continuous rally, and aim to make no mistakes.

Practice 29 – Movement Forwards and Backwards, the Forehand Overhead Fast Drop Shot and Smash, Return of Smash, Forehand and Backhand Underarm Clear.

The player stands in the midcourt. The feeder stands in the opposite midcourt and hits high serves (1) to the rearcourt. The player moves back to the rearcourt, hits a forehand overarm fast drop shot (2) and returns to the midcourt. The feeder blocks (3) to the forecourt. The player moves from the midcourt, lunges into the forecourt, plays am underarm clear (4) to the opposite rearcourt and then returns to the midcourt. The feeder plays a fast drop shot (5) to the midcourt. The player blocks to the forecourt (6) and remains in the midcourt. The feeder clears (7) high to the rearcourt. The player moves back to the rearcourt and hits a forehand overarm fast drop shot to repeat the sequence.

Conditions:
Rally for 2 minutes. Turn fast drop shots into smashes as proficiency improves.

Coaching points:
The hitting actions are tap, push and whip. The feeder blocks to either side of the player's forecourt. They play a continuous rally and aim to make no mistakes.

Practice 30 – Movement and the Forehand and Backhand Drives

The player stands in the midcourt. The first feeder (F1) stands in forecourt, and the second feeder (F2) stands in the midcourt. The first feeder (F1) hand feeds shuttles to the tramlines. The player moves sideways, lunges to hit a straight forehand drive to the second feeder (F2), then recovers to the midcourt. The second feeder (F2) hits a cross-court drive to the player's backhand side. The player moves sideways, lunges to hit a straight backhand drive, and recovers to the midcourt.

Conditions:
Play three sets. In the first set the exchanges should be forehand to backhand. In the second set they should be backhand to forehand. In the third set the second feeder (F2) hits to either side of the player.

Coaching points:
The hitting action is a tap. The forehand drives are taken off the racket foot. The backhand drives are taken off either foot.

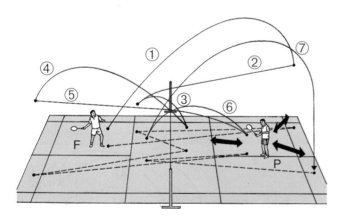

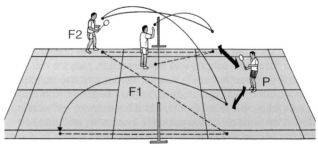

CHAPTER 10
ANALYSIS, DIAGNOSIS AND CORRECTION

To analyse is to separate a whole thing, be it a material substance, action or thought, into its elements or constituent parts. Once this process has been completed, the diagnostic work necessary to identify the cause of a weakness – or why something is successful – is simplified.

Unless this preliminary work is carried out, any effort applied to correct a fault or enhance a strength becomes a meaningless exercise. In other words you will be hitting shuttles just for the sake of it – which, if you wish to improve, is pointless.

By now you should have a clear understanding of what makes up the stroke cycle. In addition, when playing your strokes, you should be clear in your mind what type of shot you are attempting to play (a creative shot, for example) and why you chose to play it (perhaps to create space in the left rearcourt). If this is not the case, you are playing automatically.

If you are fortunate enough to have your own coach, this important aspect of the game can be left to him. Obviously a coach would be best placed to watch and analyse your work on the practice court and during a match, but if this is not possible the next best avenue open to you is help from an unqualified colleague or, failing this, self analysis. If you own or can hire a video camera the analysis can be done instantly following a replay, or later off-court after scrutiny of the recording. This method is recommended because the pictures provide you with indisputable evidence of what you actually did or did not do. It is surprising how many people think they have performed a certain action when in fact they have not!

What should you be looking at and to what should you be applying thought? A stroke has two features: the *action* (how the technique is performed) and the *outcome* (where the shuttle goes and the effect on your opponents). Sometimes the action can be lacking in technique but the outcome is one of complete success. In such cases the question 'Why bother to change the technique?' comes to mind. If the action was a stroke used very infrequently we could support the argument to leave well alone, but as this eventuality is unlikely in badminton we do have to consider other important criteria.

In comparison to other racket sports the game is relatively easy to play, so long rallies are common. For this reason experienced coaches apply certain criteria when judging the action and outcome. In judging the former they

look for economy of effort, simplicity and fluency; in the latter for accuracy, consistency and effectiveness.

With knowledge of the stroke cycle and the purpose of the stroke clear in your mind, and aware of the difference between the action and the outcome, you should now be confident enough to carry out a technical analysis of your stroke production.

TECHNICAL ANALYSIS OF: *The forehand overhead clear*

	OK	NOT OK	REMARKS
READY POSITION	✓		
TRAVEL PHASE:			
Starting	✓		
Stopping	✓		
STROKE CYCLE:			
Racket start position	✓		
Racket preparation		✗	*Shoulders square to net*
Hitting phase: push/tap/whip	✓		
point of impact		✗	*Too far forward*
Racket recovery	✓		
Movement to new base	✓		
OUTCOME:			
Shuttle flight		✗	*Too low*
Position		✗	*Short of rearcourt*

DIAGNOSIS: *Racket shoulder not pulled back. Player square to net.*
SOLUTION: *Correct and groove the throwing action. Revise point of impact.*
CORRECTIVE MEASURE: *Practice 1: Shadow of throwing action. 3 reps of 5 in static position followed by 3 of 5 with travel phase. Practice 2: High serve to player who moves to rearcourt behind the shuttle. Player allows shuttle to drop assessing intended point of impact. Practice 3: High serve to player who carries out the complete stroke cycle.*

Fig 66   Sample technical analysis sheet

Fig 68   *Weight transfer to the non-racket leg and the racket moving round to the back of the head demonstrated by Kim Ji-Hyun (Korea).*

Tumble Net Shots

You will recall producing a basic net shot from close to the net by allowing the shuttle just to bounce off the racket face. If you quickly move the racket head horizontally away from you (as if posting a letter) and slice under the bottom of the shuttle, you will achieve a tumble net shot – forecourt to forecourt. Your opponent will be reluctant to respond until the shuttle corrects itself and the base of the shuttle becomes available for hitting in the normal manner.

Another way to produce a shuttle that tumbles can also be employed when the opponent has played a shot into the forecourt directly in front of you. Using either a forehand or backhand grip, move the racket head quickly and horizontally to slice across the base of the shuttle. The shuttle will spin and pass over the net if you have moved your racket head upwards during the hit phase. It will also be of help if you remember to hold the racket lightly in the fingers and almost caress the base of the shuttle to achieve the spin.

Sliced Forehand Overhead Drop Shots

Cross-Court Sliced Drop Shots

Revise the basic throwing action and complete a series of straight drop shots, concentrating your thoughts on flat face hitting. To achieve a sliced cross-court drop shot – from the rear of the right midcourt to your opponent's right forecourt – supinate the forearm (turn it outwards) during the hitting phase of the stroke cycle so that the racket face meets the side of the shuttle base at an angle. At first the shuttle may well fall short of the net, but if you increase the power of your swing it should carry over into your opponent's court. The desired effect is that the opponent believes a faster and straighter shot is being attempted.

Reversed Sliced Drop Shots

A reversed sliced shot – from the rear of the left midcourt to your opponent's left forecourt – is achieved by pronating the forearm (turning it inwards) during the hitting phase of the stroke cycle. The racket arm goes across in front of you and again the face of the racket meets the shuttle at an angle. The desired effect is the same but the shot is more deceptive because the recipient sees the racket head go one way while the shuttle travels in the opposite direction.

Sliced Returns of the Smash

Initially it is best to perform this sliced return to a fast drop shot. Ask your coach or partner to direct his shots straight at you or slightly to your non-racket side. Using a backhand grip first tap the shuttle back over the net with a flat face hit. Once this feels comfortable, pronate your forearm to angle the racket face upwards so that a sliced shot is achieved. With practice you can apply deception by generating a fast racket head speed (as though returning the shuttle to the rearcourt) while using the slice, which takes all the pace off the shuttle and directs it into the forecourt.

Figs 69–71   Flat face, cross court and reversed slice overhead hitting

Fig 69   Flat face for straight overhead shots.

Fig 70   Forearm supinated to angle the racket face for cross court shots.

Fig 71   Forearm pronated to angle the racket face for reversed cross court shots

Advanced Movement

Jumping

In badminton you can jump voluntarily for a specific reason, or be forced to jump for fear of losing the point or being placed in an unfavourable situation. Whatever the case, the aim of the jump will be to gain height, gain distance or help you achieve balance.

Jumping vertically for height is normally used in conjunction with the smash. It enables you to take the shuttle earlier than normal and can also help you to achieve a steeper trajectory. To jump for height you must load the quadriceps by flexing the knees and pressing downwards into the floor. You then push upwards to lift your frame off the ground and take your heels behind you. When in flight take the racket shoulder back as you will be hitting the shuttle during the time you are off the ground.

Distance jumping can take you from the midcourt into the forecourt for a net kill (take off from one foot and land on the other) or to the side of the court (take off from one foot and land on two feet) to smash a shuttle down before it falls too low and becomes the subject of a drive.

Jumping from one foot to the other to help you achieve balance is known as scissor-jumping. This technique is used when receiving a flick serve or when playing a round-the-head shot. Having taken off facing the net, with the non-racket leg leading, you must throw the racket leg forwards during flight and land with this leg leading and the other to the rear. On landing the legs should be about 3ft (1m) apart to create a firm base and good balance, which are necessary before you move off to a new position.

Landing

Having jumped for height you need to absorb the shock to the joints on landing. As you land on two feet, flex the knees to cushion the impact as you meet the ground and keep your head up. This is called a deep knees landing.

Landing on completion of a jump for distance calls for a bounce on landing as it is unlikely that you can land and stop still on balance on the spot. So, having landed on two feet with flexed knees, make a small extra low bounce upwards on both feet before moving quickly off in the direction of a now base

Figs 72–73   The alterations made to the racket head to produce a sliced return

Fig 72   Flat face return of smash.

Fig 73   Forearm pronated to angle the racket face for a sliced return.

Fig 77   Jump smashes – no problem for Indonesia's Heryonto Arbi.

Figs 74–76   Jumping for height to perform a forehand overhead smash

Fig 74   Still on the way up preparing to strike the shuttle.

Fig 75   On the way down after the shuttle has been struck.

Fig 76   Deep knees landing.

PART 3

TACTICS

CHAPTER 12

SINGLES

Why is it that great singles champions do not appear on the champions' roster for competitive doubles? Is it because the singles game differs from doubles to such an extent that a player who is proficient in both disciplines does not exist?

One of the attractions of badminton is that it has something for everyone, irrespective of age. It also has variety because the singles game is vastly different from level doubles and the mixed is different again. A good singles player is often like a fish out of water when asked to play doubles, and the converse is also true. As your own game develops a preference for one or the other will come to the fore.

Within the thousands of clubs affiliated to the Badminton Association of England, doubles is the main game. This is not necessarily by the choice of the players, but because of insufficient court time. A game of singles is fitted in on that rare occasion before the club night starts or towards the end of the evening when the majority have left for home. Perhaps this is one of the reasons why British players feature much lower in world rankings for singles than for doubles.

The strokes you play in badminton are the means of carrying out your tactics. In doubles, a weakness in your strokes can sometimes be hidden or overcome. In singles this is much more difficult to achieve. You owe it to yourself to become proficient in all your strokes if only to increase the chances of winning your singles games. You should strive to be able to hit the shuttle from anywhere to anywhere on the singles court.

Table 2 (in Chapter 8) shows three types of shot – creative, 'hit and hope' and attempted winner. What the table does not show is information regarding when to play them. If it were possible to identify an ideal time to play all your shots, and you were in a position to do so, you would surely gain the upper hand. However, because of the ever changing situation and unexpected occurrences, life on a badminton court is not that simple. But with a little thought you can go some way towards finding out when to play your shots. To do this you need to master some basic principles.

First, at any time during a rally you are in either a favourable or unfavourable situation. Second, whenever you play a stroke you can do one of five things: go for a winner, try to produce something you want, give your opponent something he wants, make an error, or play a 'nothing' shot (one that does not win the rally for you or give any initiative to your opponent). Hence, if for example you are in the middle of the midcourt with the shuttle high above you (a favourable situation), you ought to go for a winner. Conversely, if you are in the rearcourt with the shuttle at knee height on your non-racket side (an unfavourable situation) you would be foolish to go for a winner; is far better to play a 'nothing' shot.

The Serve

High Serves

A high serve gives the attack to your opponent but it also moves him away from the centre of the court and into an area from which he is less of a threat. If he smashes from the rearcourt you should be able to cope with what may well be a flat return. If he is sensible, his returns from this area will be drop shots and clears to your forecourt, midcourt and rearcourt. So, you must develop a high serve of impeccable length and look briefly at your opponent's feet to check if it has reached the baseline area. On completion of your high serve, you should adopt a base position that is equidistant in terms of time from any likely reply.

Low Serves

Low serves are becoming more common in the modern singles game. These are played to prevent the receiver who has a powerful smash from gaining the initiative or in the hope that they will force a lift from the receiver. With practice you can master a deceptive low serve by going through the motions of a high serve before slowing the action down just before impact to push the shuttle low over the net. However, if your speed off the mark or movement backwards is lacking, stick to high serves until this improves sufficiently.

Flick Serves

Flick serves are not usually seen in singles but that is not to say that there is no place for them. Used with discretion, they can gain some initiative for you, particularly if you use several low serves to entice the receiver forwards before introducing a disguised flick serve.

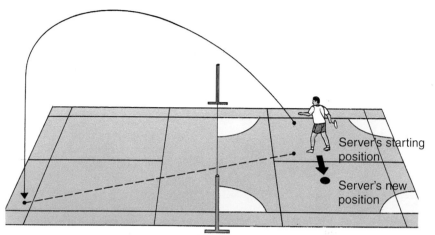

Fig 78 *Example of a high serve from the right service court showing the server's base areas before and after playing the stroke. The server's new base is equidistant from the hitting zone of each of the four shaded areas, based on the time the shuttle would take to reach them. Key: 1 High serve, 2 Server's starting base, 3 server's new base.*

Drive Serves

Once again the key word here is discretion. As the receiver usually stands well back from the front service line, drive serves do not usually achieve much advantage. However, some success is often achieved if the drive serve is used as a surprise tactic after an interruption in the play, for example a change of shuttle or change of ends at the start of a new game.

The Return of Serve

Returns to the High Serve

High serves present the receiver with three options: a clear, a smash or a drop shot. Once the high serve has been delivered your first task should be to assess its quality. If the high serve has sent you deep into the rearcourt you are advised to play a drop shot or clear to the forecourt or rearcourt before moving immediately to a new base. If the length of the

high serve is poor, the opportunity to smash presents itself and this should be uppermost in your thoughts.

Returns to the Low Serve

Low serves allow the receiver only two options: a return to the forecourt or a lift to the rearcourt. Which is the best shot to choose is debatable. The response to the forecourt may produce a lift for you to hit down but you run the risk of hitting into the net, and if the shot is of poor quality the server will move in to kill the shuttle.

The element of risk in a lift to the rearcourt is reduced somewhat but if you lift the shuttle high, your opponent will have ample time to move back to address the shuttle and hit down. Therefore a shallow clear to the backhand side of the opponent's rearcourt is perhaps the most sensible option as this will protect your own backhand area of the rearcourt and could well produce a weak shot from your opponent direct to your racket side.

Fig 79 *Possible returns to a high service.*

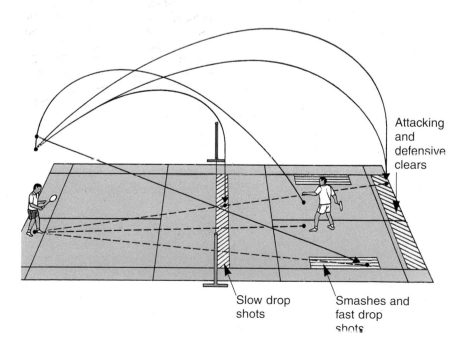

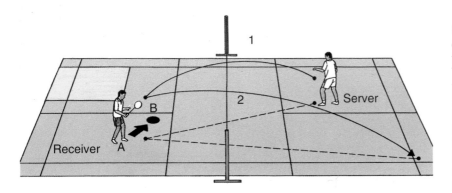

Fig 80   Example of a shallow return of a low serve to the right-handed server's left rearcourt. Areas considered 'safe' for the receiver are shaded. Key: 1 low service, 2 return of low serve, (A) receiver's starting base, (B) receiver's new base.

General Play in Singles

When some players tackle a game of singles they often forget the obvious, that the singles court is narrower than the doubles area. Therefore, it will pay you to remember when playing singles that you should exploit the length of the court more than the width and try to move your opponent up and down the full distance more frequently than from side to side.

In terms of technique, the degree of difficulty in the production of quality rearcourt backhand shots for badminton differs greatly from the forehand. Forehands are much easier to master and the players who

can perform a backhand overhead clear from the rearcourt to a good length are in a minority. For this reason alone it makes sense to find out very early in the game the quality of your opponent's backhand from the baseline area. If, as is likely, it is far weaker than his forehand equivalent, it would certainly pay to direct many of your shots to the back of the court on his non-racket side. He may well be attempting similar moves himself, so you must be ready for this and make every attempt to move quickly around the court so that the need to play backhand overhead shots is avoided as often as possible.

Where movement on the singles court is concerned, there are some occasions when you should stand still after playing a shot, but these instances are rare and in the main if you try to imagine that you are joined by a length of elastic to a post that is secured centrally on the court, it may serve to remind you to pull yourself back towards the centre after each shot. In this way a principle of hit and move will be created and your base will never be too far away from the centre of the midcourt.

USEFUL TIP

If you notice that your opponent is tired use it to your advantage. Serve as soon as you can and consider the advantage of deliberately prolonging the rallies.

Attacking in Singles

Before you can attack you need to create the opportunity to do so, and this calls for the application of tactics. The attack will be achieved by forcing your opponent to lift the shuttle high into the air, by getting the shuttle behind him (so that at best he can scramble the shuttle upwards weakly towards the net) or by moving him into a particular area of court so that a large space is left unattended. The main strokes you require to gain the attack are the smash, the attacking clear, net shots and the slow and fast drop shots.

The Smash

If you have cultivated a powerful smash on the practice court by all means use it during your singles game. But use it sensibly, at the right time and in the knowledge that it is physically demanding to keep producing it. Placement is just as important as power and the position on court from which you play it also requires consideration. Smashes played from the rearcourt area will have lost much of their power by the time they reach your opponent and they will also be flatter than those played from the midcourt. Add to this the fact that the return of your smash could be back into your court before you have recovered to the ready position and you will understand the need to reserve your smash for when you are on balance and when a constructive response is unlikely.

The Attacking Clear

As both players exploit the length of the court, underarm and overarm clears will feature prominently during the rallies. An attacking clear should reach the same spot in the rearcourt as a defensive clear. It deprives the opponent of time and is often employed in a deceptive manner after the opponent is seen to be anticipating a stroke that sends the shuttle to an area that is in front of him.

The key to success for the attacking overhead clear is bringing forward the point of impact so that the shuttle is despatched on a much lower trajectory than in the defensive clear. Experienced players with strong fingers, wrists and forearms can perform attacking clears with a tap action. These are often referred to as punch clears.

Underarm clears are usually played from the forecourt area, and if you can execute them with as little back swing as possible so much the better. Initially you may wish to draw your opponent forwards towards the net before tapping a shallow clear over his head to the rearcourt. Attacking clears are a very useful tool for your singles game but if they are not successful they will usually be met with a powerful smash from within the midcourt.

Net Shots

A well placed net shot will deprive your opponent of the chance to attack and as a bonus it could well help you gain the initiative during the rally. The key to success is to take the shuttle early; the sooner you play the shot the earlier your opponent is forced to respond. To deprive your opponent of time is a useful objective when playing singles. In addition to being early to the shuttle, always try of make contact with the shuttle when it is as high as possible.

If you manage to play a successful shot that falls close to the net, recover into a forward attacking stance and remain in the forecourt area ready to pounce on another net response by your opponent. You can do this in the knowledge that if he tries to clear to your rearcourt, if your net shot was of good quality he will have to lift the shuttle very high to achieve any depth. You will then have ample time

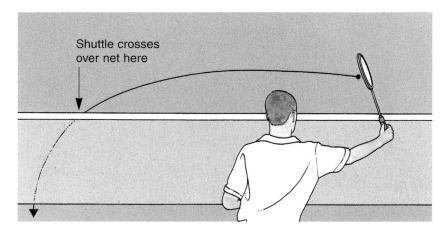

Fig 81 *Holding the racket in the backhand grip for a 'forehand' cross court net shot. The shuttle is struck with the forehand side of the racket face.*

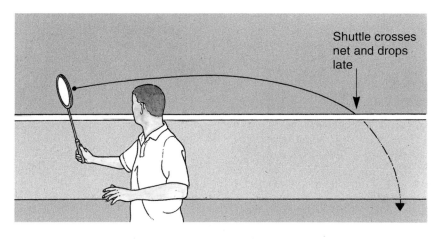

Fig 82 *Holding the racket in the pan handle grip for a 'backhand' cross court net shot. The shuttle is struck with the rear of the racket face.*

to get back behind the shuttle to play your next shot.

Cross-court net shots (forecourt to forecourt) should be played only when you have manoeuvred your opponent to the extremities of the court. The aim of a cross-court net shot is to keep the shuttle on your side of the net for as long as possible before it passes into your opponent's court. This is achieved by creating the correct angle on the racket face. Play cross-court net shots from the racket side with a backhand grip and cross-court net shots from the non-racket side with a pan handle grip.

Drop Shots

The drop shot should not be seen as a reliable means by which you win the rally. It is a creative shot and in singles you should include it only with a clear vision of what you are attempting to achieve.

Slow drop shots are an excellent tool for singles, particularly at beginner level. By playing them you are hoping to force your opponent into lifting the shuttle high into the air and create space behind him. As the shuttle takes a longer period of time to cross the net, you should be able to recover to a new base in plenty of time to cope with whatever stroke your opponent next puts your way. The decision to play the slow drop in a game should not be taken lightly.

Only if you are good on the practice court should you play it because there is no room for error and it does put pressure on you to hit to what is a relatively small area. As your standard increases you will meet players who are quick on their feet and able to read these shots. They will move to the net at speed to dab the shuttle down for a winner. In producing the shot your body language and throwing action must be made to look the same as for the overhead clear.

Fast drop shots are normally directed towards the side tramlines in the midcourt. As this is to the side of a centrally based opponent, it is normally within his reach. The main aim of the shot is to move your opponent to one side of the court and open up the other. Therefore, your shots should be crisp and well directed so that the shuttle reaches the target area quickly.

Defending in Singles

A sound defence is a fundamental aspect to successful singles play. To have the ability to be able to return the shuttle with regularity from a defensive position is a skill well worth developing.

Initially you will be content to defend by retrieving in the best way possible and with little thought. As time progresses and your standard improves, you will recognize a need to be more constructive with your defence and to try to turn defence into attack as you retrieve. The shots you will require when defending are the defensive overhead and underarm clears and the return of smash.

Clears

The aim in carrying out these defensive strokes is to move your opponent to the rearcourt if he is not already there and to gain time. Therefore to be of any use, defensive clears must achieve perfect length and lots of height. While clears to your opponent's backhand side have an obvious tactical benefit, if you become stereotyped in your play your opponent will eventually make provision for this by making his base closer to this area. If you hit the shuttle high enough you can afford to walk back to your base before settling down in anticipation of the next shot.

Returning the Smash

You will be surprised just how many players are beaten psychologically the moment their opponent shapes up to perform a smash. Quite often players forget that they have a racket and the net to help them recover from a position of defence.

You should consider where to make your base with regard to the position of your opponent and the power of his smash. The further away from the net he is, the nearer to the forecourt you should be and the closer you are to the net the higher your racket should be in relation to the top of the net.

Once in your base position, you should adopt the appropriate stance to suit the situation. As you prepare to receive the shot, you should decide where you want to direct your return. Failure to do this will result in an automatic reaction shot, which is usually a weak lift to the middle of the midcourt.

You will of course find out for yourself the physical demands of carrying out several successive smashes. With this in mind and the confidence and ability to direct high returns of the smash back to the rear of the midcourt or the rearcourt, you may consider inviting your opponent to wear himself out with a series of smashes.

Singles is a physically demanding game in which your technical expertise in stroke production will be put to the test. To be a successful singles player you will need to be fit, patient and fully aware of the situation that you find yourself in at any one time during the match. You should avoid what is a natural tendency – going for winners too early – and probe your opponent's armoury to find his likes and dislikes.

CHAPTER 13

LEVEL DOUBLES

Now that you have begun to master the strokes you should have the confidence to participate in a game of level doubles. The term level doubles is used to define either the men's or women's doubles game. The aim of this chapter is to cover the court positions of all four players during the following phases of a doubles game:

- The start
- When attacking
- When defending

> **USEFUL TIP**
>
> Encourage your partner at all times. Visible signs of discontent will do nothing for the team.

Before stepping on to the court, time spent considering some of the most important aspects of doubles, and the basic tactics associated with it, will help you gain early enjoyment of this fascinating discipline of badminton instead of periods of frustration and confusion.

Compensation, Attack and Defence

Doubles is a team game. Unless you keep out of each other's way and work as a team you will not be able to cover the whole of the court adequately and problems will arise. In simple terms, the two players in a team should imagine that they are attached to one another by a length of string about 7ft (2m) long that should become taut immediately after the serve has been

delivered and remain so until the end of the rally. For example, if your partner moves back into the rearcourt to play a stroke, you should move to a position near the forecourt to cover any of the opponents' likely replies to that area. You would do this despite not knowing what shot your partner will attempt to play; this move is one of compensation or counterbalance. By doing this there is every possibility that the imaginary piece of string will stay taut, both players will remain apart and all areas of the court will be covered.

If one of the opposing pair has lifted the shuttle into the air above the net on your side of the court, giving you the opportunity to hit the shuttle downwards, you should consider yourselves to be in a position from which you could attack.

If you have lifted the shuttle into the air above the net on your opponents'

Player	Starting Position	Reasons
Server	Front of midcourt close to centre line	So the server can move quickly to deal with any response to the forecourt after delivery of a low serve, and to establish an early presence in the forecourt and pressurize the receiver into lifting the shuttle into the air.
Server's partner	One pace behind server astride the centre line	To protect the midcourt behind the server, and to be equidistant from both sides of the midcourt and rearcourt.
Receiver	As near to front service line as is comfortable	To meet the serve as early possible so that the return may be hit down, and to pressurize the server into serving high.
Receiver's partner	Two paces behind the receiver, close to the centre line	To observe the length of the high serves and call out if necessary, and to cover the midcourt and rearcourt if the receiver remains in the forecourt.

Table 0   Starting positions for level doubles.

Fig 83   Positions at the start of the game.

side of the court, giving your opponents the opportunity to hit the shuttle downwards, you should consider yourselves to be in a position from which you may have to defend.

The Serve

Aces (winning serves that the receiver fails to touch) are a rarity in badminton, as the laws force the server to hit the shuttle upwards. Therefore the quality and placement of the serve become important in gaining the initiative as early as possible at the start of the rally.

No two games are the same, and while high serves may prove successful in one game they could be your downfall in another. Therefore it would be unwise for a coach to stipulate which of the four serves to use; it is for the player on court to decide as you take up position. The choice will be influenced by many things but the main points to consider are as follows:

- The receiver's playing standard – beginner or established player? Weak or strong smash?

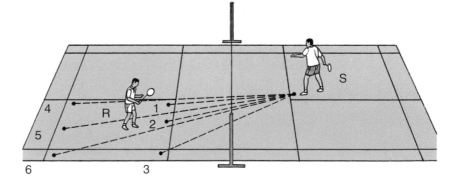

Fig 84   Direction of the serve. The laws governing the serve restrict you to serving towards the diagonally opposite service area. The diagram shows the general areas to which the four types of serve are normally directed from the right-hand court to a right-handed receiver. Key: 1, 2 and 3 low serves; 4, 5 and 6 high serves; 4 and 6 drive or flick serves.

- Position and stance of the receiver – does he stand close to the service line, poised with knees flexed ready to move in any direction? Where is his racket?
- The score – is the game at a crucial stage, such as match point? Do you have a comfortable lead? Is this the first or deciding third game?
- Your standard of serving – good or erratic? Has it been up to your normal standard during the early stages of the game?
- Position of receiver's partner – does he encroach into the receiver's service court?

Inexperienced players will serve and wait for a response. The more seasoned player will serve and anticipate the direction of the reply. Quite often you can gain some initiative by encouraging a particular response or by preventing your opponents from dominating the early part of the rally.

Figs 85 and 86 show two examples of how the direction of your serve can influence the rally. Never serve simply to get the shuttle into play. Every stroke you play has a consequence and deserves thought, and this is especially so with the serve.

COURT DIAGRAMS

The players' positions on court diagrams are shown as follows:

S	server
SP	server's partner
R	receiver
RP	receiver's partner

The Return of Serve

The Low Serve Returns

When returning the low serve many placements are possible. The degree of difficulty and margin for error required in the production of the chosen stroke and direction vary greatly. Table 4 and Fig 87 list some of the more common returns. After assessing the risk factors involved in producing each one, a merit mark on a scale of 1 (low) to 10 (high) has been assigned.

The receiver is unlikely to know the type and direction of the serve until after the shuttle has been despatched. Therefore, any plan he may have to direct his return to a specific area of the court may prove difficult to achieve if you keep him guessing. This explains the need to be flexible in your approach to this aspect of the doubles game and to understand fully the advantages and disadvantages of returning serves to different areas of the court.

Returns to the High Serve

After delivering the low serve, movement by the server's team is minimal. By comparison, after a high serve has been delivered – and assuming they know about defence – your opponents will move into a defensive formation. This formation creates clear areas of responsibility for each player and alters dramatically the merit marks awarded in Table 4. For example, low serve return No. 3 (which enticed both the server and the server's partner to move to the same shuttle and gained 8 merit marks) no longer causes confusion as it becomes the undisputed responsibility of the server's partner; the mark of 8 should be reduced to 5.

Study the paragraphs on defending formations and note what the new positions of the server and the server's partner would be following the high serve. Assign your own revised merit marks to all eight returns. Early in the game, you and your partner should watch how your opponents react when called upon to defend. The formation they adopt will influence your choice of return to the high serve.

The Drive Serve Returns

Usually, drive serves are delivered to create a response to an area that your opponents favour or make provision for. This serve often produces a spontaneous reaction and a shot that is played without thought. You must guard against this and always try to play a return that will be of benefit to your team. The server may unknowingly forecast the delivery of a drive serve by moving backwards and outwards from his normal serving position to create an angle for himself. Watch out for this and also for a much

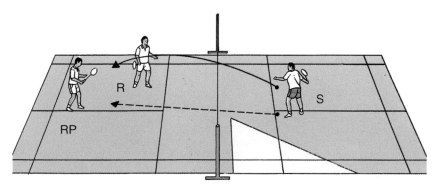

Fig 85   Example 1 (encouraging a particular response). A drive serve directed from the left-hand court to the right-handed receiver whose partner is standing astride the centre service line. This promotes twofold uncertainty in that the receiver has to decide whether the serve will go out of court at both the back or sides of the court. The result is usually a tentative approach to the shuttle for fear of hitting his partner with his racket and a reaction shot to the shaded area.

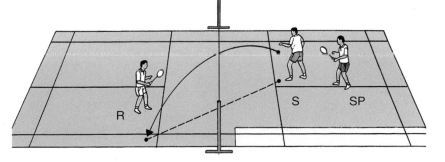
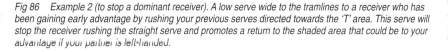

Fig 86   Example 2 (to stop a dominant receiver). A low serve wide to the tramlines to a receiver who has been gaining early advantage by rushing your previous serves directed towards the 'T' area. This serve will stop the receiver rushing the straight serve and promotes a return to the shaded area that could be to your advantage if your partner is left-handed.

Return number	Type of shot	Intention	Risks	Merit mark
1	Push to centre forecourt	Give server no angle; pressure server to lift	May hit into net or too high	9
2	Push to side forecourt	Move server to side forecourt; force server to lift	May hit into net or out at side	7
3	Push to side midcourt	Move server and server's partner to side midcourt for same shuttle	May hit out at side	8
4	Tap to body of server's partner	Give server's partner no angle and force weak return	May hit out at back	10
5	Tap to rearcourt	Move server's partner to side of rearcourt and force weak backhand response	May hit out at back; may hit out at side	6
6	Tap to forecourt	Move server to side forecourt and force server to lift	May hit into net or out at side; server may cut off	5
7	Tap to midcourt	Move server and server's partner to side midcourt for same shuttle	May hit out at side; server may cut off	4
8	Tap to rearcourt rearcourt	Move server's partner to side	May hit out at side; may hit out at back	5

Table 4   Returns to the low serve in level doubles.

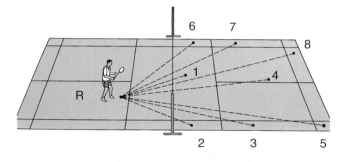

Fig 87   Returns of the low serve.

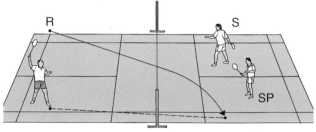

Fig 88   Example of a return of a high serve to the midcourt. This return is clearly the responsibility of the server's partner, who moved to this position after S had served.

faster arm movement as he brings the racket forward to strike the shuttle.

Drive serves from the server's right-hand court down the non-racket side of the right-handed receiver are the most common.

The Flick Serve Returns

To return a good flick serve is difficult, if not impossible. If the shuttle has travelled to a position behind you, your opponent has achieved his aim, and to say that you are in trouble is an understatement. If the flick serve has met with only partial success, try to clear the shuttle as high and as deep as possible to your opponents' backhand rearcourt.

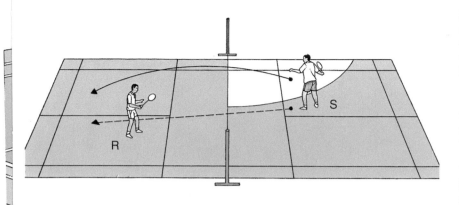

Fig 89 Example of a drive serve from the server's right-hand court down the non-racket side of the right-handed receiver. The shaded portion is the expected area of return. A drive serve will continue to rise after it passes over the net, so as you can move immediately after the shuttle has been struck, try to reply to this serve with a forehand round-the-head stroke, to an area on the server's non-racket side.

Quite often players forecast their intention to carry out a flick serve by quickening the racket arm movement early in the swing, moving their body upwards and in some cases by telling their partner.

Court Positions as a Doubles Team

There are numerous systems that can be operated to meet the ever changing situations that arise on a level doubles court. This part of the chapter covers the most basic formations that are necessary in order that you and your partner can operate safely as a team with some general

Figs 90–92 Attacking formations

Fig 90 Front and back attack. In this formation the shuttle is high in the rearcourt area being addressed by the striker. His partner is in the area of the 'T' dominating the forecourt.

Fig 91 Channel attack. The shuttle is now high in the midcourt following a poor quality clear. All emphasis will now be applied to the straight defender in an effort to win the rally with a powerful smash or, failing this, force a weak lift that the forecourt player can kill.

Fig 92 Wedge attack. The shuttle remains high in the midcourt. This formation is useful when your opponents can cope with the straight smashes and have been returning the shots with low cross-court replies. This formation now enables the front player to cut off this response.

CHAPTER 14

MIXED DOUBLES

Where the more experienced players are concerned, the mixed doubles game is probably the most popular of the five disciplines of badminton 'down at the club'. Many of the younger players tolerate the odd game of mixed but they much prefer level doubles.

Mixed doubles is undoubtedly more popular with the women than the men; some men treat it as a chance to play mixed men's drive singles and scold the woman partner who dares to intrude. Coaches will discuss the tactics of the mixed game at length, and married couples who play mixed doubles together without arguing are a rarity. All these observations contribute to what makes the mixed game so very intriguing and attractive.

The aim of this chapter is to cover the court positions of all four players during the following phases of a mixed doubles game:

- The start
- When attacking
- When defending

The players' positions on court diagrams are shown as follows:

L	woman
M	man
LS	woman server
MS	man server
LR	woman receiver
MR	man receiver
- - - - - - - >	direction of shuttle
———————>	movement of player

Compensation, Attack and Defence

In mixed doubles the same principles to those covered in the level doubles game for compensation, attack and defence apply. You should try to operate in a balanced format, as a team and consider yourselves to be attacking when able to hit down and defending when you have lifted the shuttle into the air.

If the basic principles of mixed doubles are the same as those applied to level doubles, what differences are there and why are they required? The main differences are the starting positions of the woman when the man serves and receives, and her particular area of responsibility in the defensive formation of the team when they have lifted the shuttle high into the air above the net. The differences are required because the team comprises a male and female whose attributes for badminton differ to such an extent that two distinctly separate roles are required.

KEY POINT

During mixed doubles play it is tactically sound to keep cross-court shots to a minimum.

Attributes and Roles of Mixed Doubles Players

As you gain in experience in doubles you will be able to identify your own style of play, strengths and

weaknesses. Some players read the game well and become known for their tactical prowess, while others gain reputations for having a powerful smash or accurate drop shots. Players can be identified as either set-up players, hit players or in some cases both.

KEY POINT

In mixed doubles a woman with a good low serve is worth her weight in gold.

In a doubles pair it is unlikely that two set up players or two hit players together would gain as much success as a team containing one of each category. The player with the deft touch and guile would probably feel more at ease in the forecourt than the rearcourt and the hit player would be of little use to the team if he were trapped in the forecourt and did not have the opportunity to use his smash. Therefore, the wise team will play to its strengths and protect its weaknesses by adopting a style that suits the individual attributes of the pair.

As a general rule (and there are exceptions) women are much better set up players than their male counterparts. This is because they are more patient, have better touch and are far better net players. Men are usually more explosive and powerful and are not as subtle.

Taking these different attributes of the male and female player into consideration, it is usual and sensible for the woman to take on the set up

Player	Starting position	Reasons
Woman server	Front of midcourt close to centre line.	So she can move quickly to deal with any response to the forecourt after delivery of a low serve.
Server's partner (man)	One pace behind the server, astride the centre line.	To protect the midcourt behind the server, and to be equidistant from both sides of the midcourt and rearcourt.
Man server	Close to centre line two paces back from front service line.	So he can move quickly to deal with any response to the midcourt or rearcourt after delivery of a low serve.
Server's partner (woman)	If the man serves left handed or is a right handed player using the backhand serve, the woman stands to the right of the 'T', otherwise she takes up position to the left.	To cover and deal with any response to the forecourt after delivery of a low serve.
Woman receiver	As near to front service line as is comfortable.	To meet the serve as early as possible so that the return may be hit down, and to pressurize the server into serving high.
Receiver's partner (man)	Two paces behind the receiver close to centre line.	To observe the length of the high serves and call out if necessary, and to cover the midcourt and rearcourt if the receiver remains in the forecourt.
Man receiver	As near to the front service line as is comfortable.	To meet the serve as early as possible so that the return may be hit down, and to pressurize the server into serving high.
Receiver's partner (woman)	If the man receives in the right hand court, the woman stands to the left of the 'T'. If the man receives in the left hand court, the woman stands to the right of the 'T'.	To assume immediate responsibility for the forecourt if her partner's return of the serve gains the attack.

Table 5   Starting positions for mixed doubles.

role and the man the hit role. This style allows the woman to concentrate her positional play within the forecourt and midcourt areas as she searches for the chance to make an opening (force a lift into the air) with tight net shots and pushes to the midcourt. The man is best placed behind her so that he can attack the shuttle that has been lifted to the rearcourt by hitting downwards as often as possible. Table 5 shows suggested starting positions for mixed doubles.

This principle that the woman is predominantly at the front of the court with the man behind forms the foundation of basic tactics for mixed doubles. The more astute reader will already have surmised that one way of weakening the team would be to reverse the roles by forcing the woman to the rearcourt in the hope that the man will compensate by moving forward into an unfamiliar mid or forecourt area.

The Serve

The main points that may influence your choice of serve in level doubles were outlined in Chapter 13. In the mixed game the same considerations should apply but the position and stance of the receiver merits particular note. When receiving serve, the majority of women have an understandable fear of moving backwards quickly and adjust their

Figs 99–101   Positions at the start of the game

Fig 99   When the woman serves from the right to the woman.

Fig 100   When the man serves from the left to the man. Note the position of the receiver's partner, to the right of the 'T'.

Fig 101   When the right-handed man serves backhand from the left to the man. Note the position of the server's partner, who is in front of the man on the right of the 'T'. Table 5 explains why these positions have been suggested.

stance accordingly by standing back from the front of the midcourt. While this invites a low serve to the front of the midcourt, a high serve could well be the better option because it moves the woman back deep into the midcourt away from the area that befits her role.

The man receiver who toes the front service line is gambling on being able to put away your low serve for fear of being caught with the third shot of the rally that is whipped low to his rearcourt. The answer here is to develop a low serve of supreme consistency and to sow a seed of uncertainty into the receiver's mind by occasionally serving wide to the tramlines or flick serving.

The Return of Serve

Returns to the Low Serve

With a woman dominating the forecourt in support of her male partner who is serving, the accuracy of your return of serve becomes crucial. Returns of serve that direct the shuttle across the forehand side of the woman in the forecourt should be few and far between otherwise they will be quickly cut off.

When the man returns the low serve downwards he must remember to recover to a base behind the woman as soon as possible. By doing so, if his return of serve is not an outright winner, he will be well placed to deal with shuttles lifted to the rearcourt.

Returns to the High Serve

As in the case of the returns to a high serve in level doubles, this aspect again needs to be considered in the light of how your opponents choose to position themselves as a team to defend. You will have to watch carefully to see if the woman drops back from the 'T' to defend, or whether she remains in this central position. Most established woman club players do move back to form what is often known as triangular defence. This calls for care in selecting the direction of a smash or fast drop shot.

It is generally advisable to opt for a return directed either straight down the line or between the two

Fig 102 Simon Archer (England) delivers a backhand serve while Julie Bradbury (England) is poised ready to attack any loose return.

opponents because cross-court smashes and drop shots and smashes can often be picked off by the woman. A cross-court attacking clear is well worth the effort providing it reaches the rearcourt. The penalty for playing a cross-court clear that falls short of the rearcourt will be severe: a smash is the likely response.

Court Positions as a Mixed Doubles Team

The positions on court for the mixed doubles pair following the opening serve is the subject of much discussion by players and coaches alike. There are endless post match debates concerning who should have been where, and which player should have accepted responsibility for a particular shot. A tactically sound mixed doubles pair is not created overnight and there is no instant blueprint for success. In broad terms, if the man attacks cross-court and defends straight while his

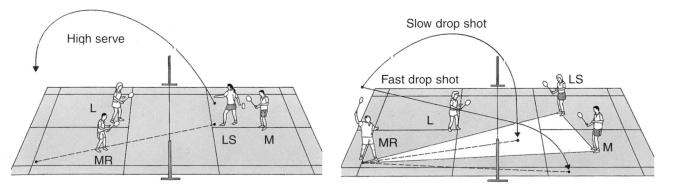

Fig 103   Example of drop shot returns to a high serve with the opposing players forming a triangular defence.

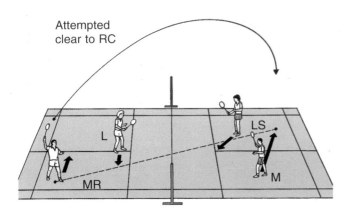

Attempted
clear to RC

L

LS

MR

M

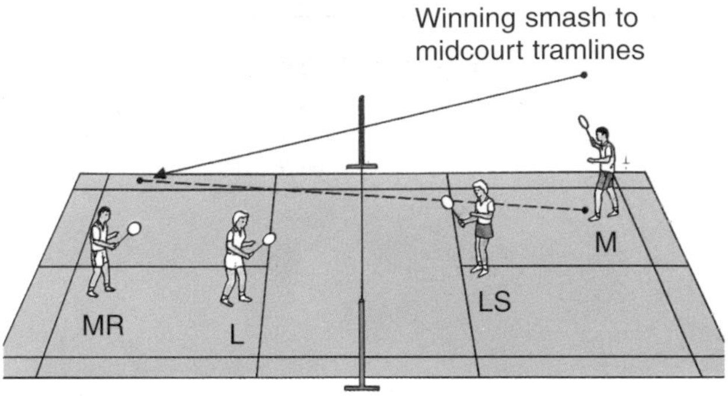

Winning smash to
midcourt tramlines

MR

L

LS

M

Fig 104   Example of an ineffective cross court clear.

woman attacks straight and defends cross-court, the team will not go too far wrong tactically, so long as their strokes are good enough to carry out the tactics.

Movement around the court to take the mixed pair into positions for attack or defence requires regular practice and discussion with regard for the players' roles. Long standing partnerships move with complete confidence in each other's ability while members of newly formed teams often duplicate their partner's movements and leave large gaps in the court. The clever mixed pair will show patience in their attempts to create attack, and if either player is called upon to cope with situations that take them out of their area of responsibility, they will strive to return there as soon as possible.

USEFUL TIP

If you communicate with your partner you will help yourself to relax and show your opponents that you are working as a team.

Figs 105–110   Attacking and defending formations

Fig 105   A typical example of both sides on the attack exchanging drives down the tramlines.

Fig 106   Attack from the right rearcourt of Team A (furthest away from camera). Team A is an attacking formation with the woman near the "T". Team B (back to camera) are defending.

Fig 107 *Attack from the left rearcourt of Team A (furthest from camera). Team A in an attacking formation. Team B (back to camera) are defending with the woman poised ready to deal with any cross court attack. Although the woman is positioned cross-court from the shuttle and to the side of her male partner, she is nearer to the net. The slightly forward position helps to prevent the opponents tempting her to move back into the rearcourt by playing a clear over her head.*

Figs 108–110 *A movement sequence showing the woman dealing with a high serve and moving into the forecourt. Note the position of the man (who has not been drawn into the forecourt) and the adjusted central position of the man after the woman has reached the 'T' area.*

PART 4

FITNESS

CHAPTER 15

PHYSICAL FITNESS

It is quite possible to play badminton without being fit. Furthermore, if your technical skills and tactical knowledge are sound, you could compete against others who are also not fit and achieve considerable success. So, why bother with any physical fitness at all? Well, for a start, by preparing your body for exercise you will be able to play the game for a longer period of time – which, assuming you participate for enjoyment, has to be a plus factor.

> **KEY POINT**
>
> Keep up your fitness. It takes a third of the time taken to get fit to become unfit again.

It is also unwise, even dangerous, to place vigorous demands on your body and system without some form of preparation. If you are a newcomer to the game and an over 35 who has done little previous physical activity, it would be foolish to rush into a game of singles. You should not play badminton to get fit – more to the point, you should get fit to play badminton!

It is not the aim of this chapter to produce superb athletes who can play badminton for hours without breaking into a sweat. The following paragraphs are intended to make you aware of how the body works and to give you some ideas of how to prepare yourself physically for badminton. Read in conjunction with Chapter 17, the information that follows will help you to reduce fatigue on court, lessen the likelihood of injury and enhance your general health and well-being.

The human body is made up of a number of rigid bones, collectively called the skeleton, which are jointed together. This skeleton is covered with hundreds of muscles that are organized in pairs so that when one muscle contracts its partner stretches. Muscles are made of fibres grouped together. There are two types of fibres – fast and slow twitch. Fast twitch fibres operate at their best when fuelled with carbohydrate whereas slow twitch fibres can function efficiently with a mixture of carbohydrate and fat. Both types function more efficiently when warmed up.

The Energy Systems

Three energy systems provide the power to produce muscle contractions:

- Anaerobic (alactic) – for single dynamic movements, such as a high serve. This system requires no oxygen to replenish the muscles.
- Anaerobic (lactic) – for repeated dynamic movements, say fast movements for over 10 seconds and up to a minute. This system requires no oxygen to replenish the muscles but produces lactic acid, a waste deposit, which has to be cleared from the muscle for it to function again.
- Aerobic – the slow twitch system used for muscular actions that last for over a minute, which is typical of a long rally in singles. This system requires oxygen to replenish the muscles.

Hence, 100m sprinters work hard to develop their anaerobic (alactic) systems, 400m runners the anaerobic (lactic) system and marathon runners the aerobic energy system. In badminton all three energy systems are utilized.

Fig 111   Ardi Wiranata displays well developed quadriceps as he performs a side lunge.

Each of us is unique; our response and attitude to fitness and training differ. Several factors contribute to how we perform and some people will make progress far quicker than others. We have all experienced the days when we feel good and those periods of time when we feel well below our best. The level of fitness you wish to achieve depends on ambition and desire. The higher your goal the more dedicated and intense the fitness programme will have to be.

Warm-Up

All training and competitive play should be preceded by a warm up. It is an essential aspect of any physical activity. The aim of doing a warm up is to prepare yourself mentally and physically for the work that follows. You will operate more efficiently if the body temperature is raised and you warm up the muscles and increase the heart rate. A simple but effective warm up for badminton should consist of the following:

- 5 minutes of continuous jogging at very slow speed
- A series of exercises to stretch the muscles
- Some fast-reaction simulation movements – perhaps shadow badminton play on court

> **KEY POINT**
>
> Before a match, after you have warmed up physically, always practise your basic strokes. Doing this helps you adjust to hall temperature, shuttle flight and general conditions.

Fig 112   Hermawan Susanto (Indonesia) shows superb flexibility in this deep lunge into the forecourt.

Getting Fitter – Developing the Energy Systems

Speed Endurance Work (Anaerobic Development)

This can be improved by interval training. Swimming, cycling, running, skipping and shadow badminton are all suitable methods of exercise for interval work. Here the player applies a work/recovery ratio to allow the muscles to remove the lactic waste deposits between each activity. The development of the alactic system requires a work ratio of 1:5. Therefore, a sprint of 50m at 100 per cent effort should be followed by a rest period of five times the time taken.

Development of the lactic system requires a work ratio of 1:2. For example, sprinting for 50m at 80 per cent effort should be followed by a rest period of twice the time taken.

Heart and Lungs Endurance Work (Aerobic Development)

This improves the efficiency of the heart and lungs and so increases the amount of oxygenated blood transported to the muscles. The aerobic system can be developed by interval training and continuous exercise. The latter is known as steady state work and is beneficial only if the intensity is such that the heart rate is increased to a sensible and realistic level.

You can monitor your temporal, radial or carotid pulse rate by placing your index and forefinger lightly in position. To take your temporal pulse place the two fingers on the temple and count the number of beats in 10 seconds before multiplying by 6 to establish beats per minute.

Use the chart shown in Fig 114 to find your ideal training zone. If you do not train with sufficient intensity to

IDEAL HEART RATE TRAINING ZONE

You can work out what your ideal heart rate training zone is according to your age by using the following formulae:

Maximum heart rate (MHR) = 220 − age

Ideal heart rate training zone = 220 − age × percentage of MHR

Example: An active 40 year old who is fit should be able to work at between 70 to 80 per cent of his MHR. His ideal heart rate training zone is calculated as:

220 − 40 = 180 × 70 per cent = 126

220 − 40 = 180 × 80 per cent = 144

The ideal training zone is between 126 and 144 beats per minute.

If you are an unfit 40 year old, subtract a further 20 beats from the 220 to establish a more suitable lower training zone:

220 − 40 − 20 = 160 × 70 per cent = 112

220 − 40 − 20 = 160 × 80 per cent = 128

The ideal training zone is now between 112 and 128 beats per minute.

---

produce a heart rate that is within the zone you will not improve your fitness level. Conversely, if you exercise too intensely you will run out of oxygen and your system will change to the anaerobic system, which operates without a need for oxygen. This is all very well but the greater the intensity of work, the less time the fuel − creatine phosphate − will last and eventually you will have to slow down or stop to refuel with oxygen.

Flexibility

If you have the opportunity to watch the top singles players you will be amazed at their flexibility. To be flexible has many advantages in badminton not least of which is the ability to stretch and reach for your opponent's well placed drop shot that he is convinced will be a winner. Being flexible will help your technique and general fitness and can

contribute to better speed and reduced fatigue. To stretch takes the muscles and joints beyond their habitual length and when done properly and regularly helps to prevent injury. Work to improve flexibility should not be started until the warm up has been completed.

Static Stretching

This is slow stretching and can be incorporated into warm up routines. A muscle will be lengthened and held in its new position for 30 seconds before slowly being released. This should be repeated three times and is often best carried out with a partner who can assist in the stretching process.

Ballistic Stretching

These are quick movements that are not held in position before contraction takes place. Only a momentary lengthening of the muscle group takes place. They are good for some speed work but as they are of a repetitive bouncing nature, they should not be included in the warm up section of your work or in leg work where the surface of the floor is absolutely solid.

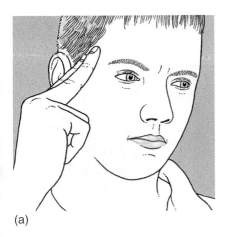
(a)

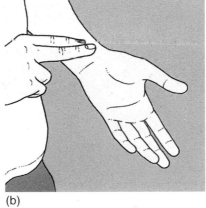
(b)

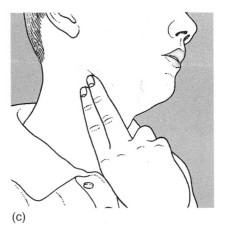
(c)

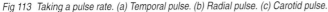

Fig 113 Taking a pulse rate. (a) Temporal pulse. (b) Radial pulse. (c) Carotid pulse.

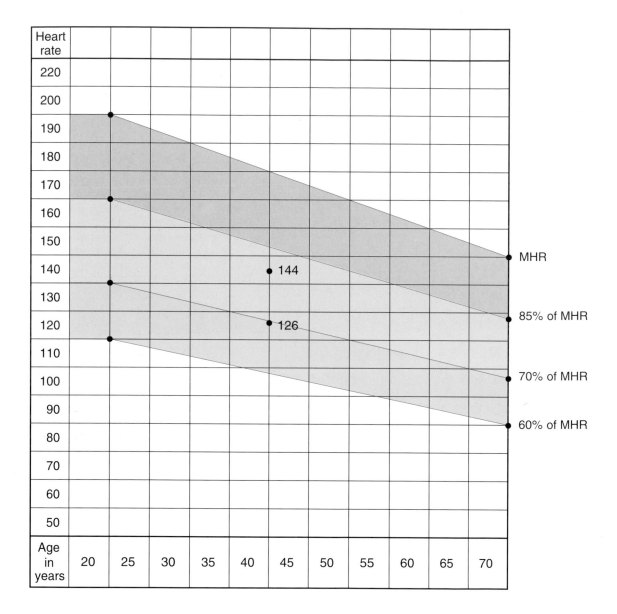

Fig 114   Use this chart to find your ideal training zone.

Warm Down

Perhaps the most neglected part of our physical training programmes is the warm down. In our haste to replenish the body with liquid refreshment before resting we often neglect the need to bring the system back down to normality once the rigors of the training or competition has been concluded.

If you continue to move the muscle groups used during the training or competitive activity slowly and rhythmically until your heart rate has returned to near normal resting rate, and follow this with a hot shower, you will reap the benefit. Stiffness and cramps will be avoided if some light exercise is undertaken to force the fluids, especially lactic acid, out of the muscles.

Figs 115–124   Examples of static stretching

The shaded areas illustrate where the stretch takes place.

Hold all positions for 30 seconds before releasing slowly. Repeat 3 times.

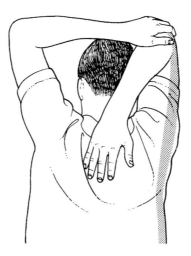

Fig 115   Shoulder stretch. Cross the elbows of one arm across the chest and press the arm into the body with the other arm. Repeat with the other arm.

Fig 116   Shoulder and back of upper arm. Pull the elbow of one arm behind your head and press downward. Repeat with the other arm.

Fig 117   Side stretch. Feet shoulder width apart. Extend one arm up and over the head, then bend sideways. Repeat for the other side.

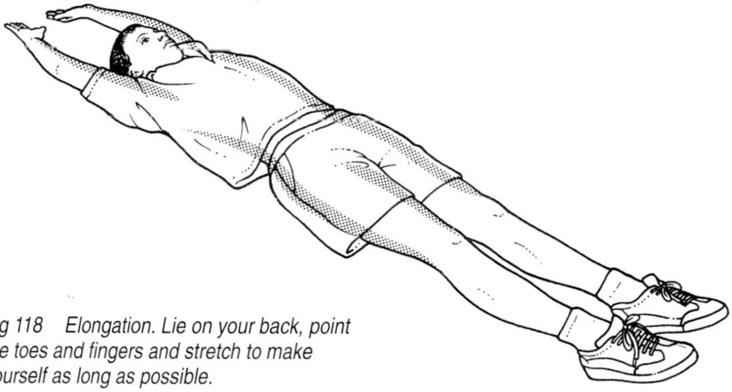

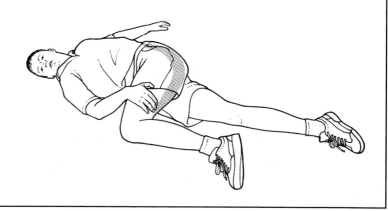

Fig 118   Elongation. Lie on your back, point the toes and fingers and stretch to make yourself as long as possible.

Fig 119   Lower back and side of hips. Bend the left leg to 90 degrees and the knee and take it over the right leg. Stretch out the left arm to keep the shoulders on the ground. Pull the left leg down with the right arm.

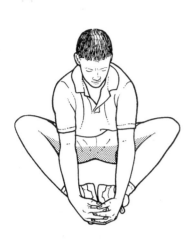

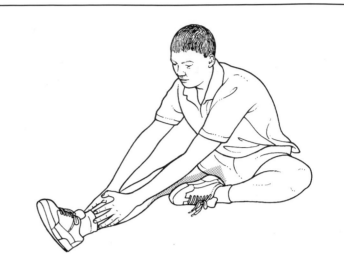

Fig 120   Groin stretch. Sit on the floor with the soles of the feet together (held by the hands). Keeping your head up bend from the hips until your feel the groin stretch.

Fig 121   Hamstrings. Extend one leg and rest the sole of the other foot against it. Bend forwards from the hips. Keep your head up. Repeat with the other leg.

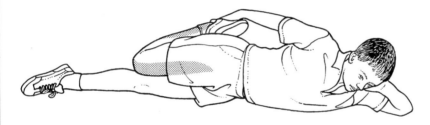

Fig 122   Quadriceps. Lie on one side and pull the ankle of the uppermost leg back towards the hip until you feel the stretch. Repeat with the other leg.

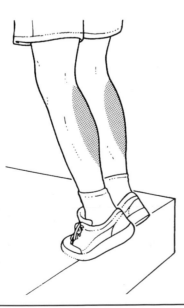

Fig 124   Calf and Achilles stretch. Take up the position as shown on a firm board or similar. Gently force the heels downwards keeping the legs straight.

Fig 123   Calf stretch. Stand as shown with one leg forward. Keeping the heel of the rear leg on the ground push against the wall. Repeat with the other leg.

Guide to Body Circuit Exercises

Press Ups

Adopt the front support position. Bend the arms to lower the chest to the floor and then straighten the arms to return to the start position. Keep your body rigid throughout and do not allow the lower back to sag. Make sure your arms are no more than shoulder width apart.

Squat Jumps

Kneel down on one knee with fingers touching the floor. Jump up high into the air and change legs so as to land and kneel on the other knee.

Sit Ups

Adopt the prone position on your back with the hands placed palms down on top of your quadriceps. Lift up the trunk and slide the hands down to touch the knees before returning to the original position.

Back Lifts

Adopt the prone position on your front with the hands clasped together behind your back. Keeping the pelvis area on the ground raise the shoulders and legs off the ground then lower to the original position.

Step Ups

Using a firm chair or bench step up and down. Lead with the left leg for half the sequence and change to the right leg for the other half.

Burpees

Adopt the standing position with hands down by your side. Crouch down to place the hands on the floor in front of you. Now jump the legs out backwards to adopt the front support position. Work in reverse to return to the original standing position. Keep the back straight throughout the movement.

Shuttle Runs

Place two markers 10m apart. Run from one to the other and lunge on to the racket foot to touch the ground at the side of each marker.

WEEKLY TRAINING PROGRAMME

Duration approximately 2 hours 50 minutes.

1. Warm up to ideal training zone.

2. Aerobic work (for heart and lung endurance). Do either *steady state work* (continuous jogging, swimming cycling or shadow badminton for 20 minutes at 60 per cent effort) or *interval work* (jogging, sprinting and walking for 20 minutes at 70 per cent effort). Work to rest ratio is 1:1 but if you find this too easy go for 2:1. Three times a week (60 minutes).

3. Anaerobic work (for speed endurance). For your lactic system: shadow badminton or run at 80 per cent effort for 30 seconds. Doing this 10 times constitutes one set. Do two sets with 60 seconds rest between repetitions and 3 minutes rest between sets 1 and 2 (10 minutes). For your alactic system: shadow badminton or run, 100 per cent effort for 10 seconds. Doing this 10 times constitutes one set. Do two sets with 50 seconds rest between repetitions and no rest between sets (4 minutes).

4. Body Circuit (remember to warm up). Do three sets of a, b or c three times a week. Do them properly, in order and as fast as you can (20 minutes).

	a	b	c
Press ups	5	10	20
Squat jumps	10	15	20
Sit ups	10	15	20
Back lifts	10	15	20
Step ups	20	30	40
Burpees	5	10	15
Shuttle runs	10	15	20

5. Flexibility; slow stretching for 10 minutes three times a week (30 minutes).

6. Warm ups and warm downs (45 minutes).

CHAPTER 16

COMMON BADMINTON INJURIES

Badminton is a non-contact sport – if you have reached a reasonable level of fitness, wear the correct shoes, warm up before playing and have correct technique, you should not expect too many injuries. As your love of the game increases, so will the frequency of your play and your level of fitness. Inevitably, therefore, there will be times when injuries occur.

It is often said that a little knowledge is dangerous, so the contents of this chapter are offered only as a guide to the badminton player. Professional medical advice should always be sought.

Blisters

These are perhaps the most niggling minor problem; they occur mostly on the heels and toes, and at times on the hands. Blisters on the feet are usually caused by ill fitting shoes or socks that rub against a particular area. The best treatment is to clean the area with an antiseptic before pricking the blister to allow the fluid to drain away. Once this has been done, leave the skin in place and cover with gauze.

Sprained Ankle

Sprains are a common traumatic injury associated with all sports where running, jumping and landing is involved. They are frustrating in that

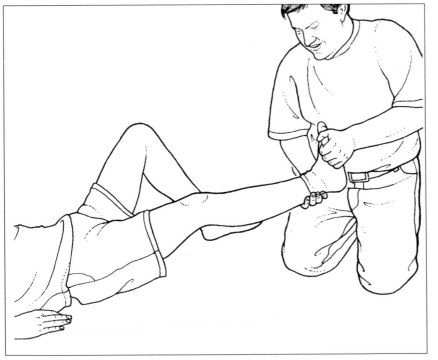

Fig 125   *Treatment of cramp in the calf muscles. Straighten the leg and move the foot upwards towards the shin. Now gently massage the affected area.*

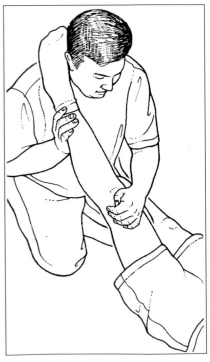

Fig 126   *Treatment of cramp in the thigh muscles. Straighten and raise the leg and with one hand on the heel raise the leg to rest on the shoulder. With the other hand, press down on the knee. Now gently massage the affected area.*

they often occur during a match and bring it to a halt. When a sprain occurs it is in your own interests to act quickly. By applying first aid as soon as is possible, the time it takes to recover can be greatly reduced.

The mnemonic RICE (*Rest, Ice, Compress, Elevate*) will help you to remember what to do in the first instance. After a minimum of 48 hours of rest, light movement to exercise the injured area should be carried out.

Tennis Elbow

This is a common injury and many racket players will be quick to tell you about the pain associated with it. In the majority of cases the cause is overuse but in some circumstances bad technique or too small a grip can be the reason. It can even be attributed to the use of shuttles with an incorrect speed.

The RICE principle will help in the initial stages but in severe cases support will be necessary to take the load off the affected area. There are numerous support bandages and splints on the market and what suits one player may not suit another. No miracle cure exists but if you can pinpoint the root cause you have every chance of preventing continual discomfort – which in extreme cases can force players to lay off racket sports for a whole season.

Calf Muscle Strain

When this occurs the player often believes that someone or something has struck the back of the leg. The cause is sudden overloading or stretching of the muscle or group of muscles. The risk of muscle strain can be minimized by completion of a thorough warm up and correct technique. The best treatment is RICE

– and care should be taken not to return to the activity too soon.

Cramp

This a painful experience in which the muscle or a group of muscles contract without warning. The onset of cramp is normally associated with fatigue. The cause can be due to a loss of salt and body fluids during sweating, or the player suddenly becoming cold. The victim experiences tightness in the area and lots of pain.

Usually, badminton players get cramp in their legs and especially in the area of the calf muscles. Treatment should include straightening of the leg (to stretch the muscles) and gently massage. Once the pain has subsided it pays to keep the legs warm by donning tracksuit trousers but in competition this may not be permitted.

CHAPTER 17

NUTRITION

A great deal of knowledge about nutrition is available and there is much to be gained by understanding the basic principles of diet. Eating is an important and obligatory part of our lives; food has a social and psychological role. For those of us who play sport it contributes to our biological and physiological well-being. Top performers need to control and monitor their diet constantly as they strive for perfection.

The higher your ambitions within badminton the more you will have to consider nutrition. Carbohydrates are the most important fuel because high reserves of glycogen delay the onset of fatigue. Your fat intake should be limited and those essential amino acids not produced naturally within the body will be obtained if you are eating a balanced diet. Further information on this interesting subject can be obtained from the National Sports Medicine Institute of the United Kingdom.

As food is required for general bodily functions, growth and repair of bone, skin and tissues, it should be regarded as a fuel. Food provides energy and where the badminton player is concerned, the main consideration should be the provision of sufficient quantities of the correct fuel. Most foods contain different nutrients. The six essential nutrients are carbohydrates, fats, proteins, vitamins, minerals and water. While all six are essential for a balanced diet, only carbohydrates, fats and proteins provide the body with energy.

Carbohydrates

Carbohydrate is stored within the liver and muscles as glycogen. Those foods that are high in carbohydrates are divided into two types:

- Simple carbohydrates – sugars, syrups, jams, confectionery, sweets, pastries, ice cream, milk drinks, cola, lemonade, fruit pies, crumbles and fruit yoghurts
- Complex carbohydrates – wholemeal products, pasta, brown rice, pulses, non-sugar-coated cereals, unsalted nuts, fresh fruit, potatoes and root vegetables

Fats

While some fats provide us with vitamins A, D and E, high intake of saturated fat may raise your blood cholesterol level and increase the chances of developing heart disease. As a fuel for the sportsman, fat is of less importance. Fats can be split into two categories:

- Saturated fatty acids – mainly found in animal fats
- Unsaturated fatty acids – mainly found in vegetables or fish

Proteins

Some proteins, which are composed of amino acids, need to be obtained direct from food while others are produced naturally by the body. Pulses, vegetables and cereals are good sources of protein, especially those that are high in carbohydrate and fibre: pulses, lentils, peas, beans, bread, potatoes and pasta. Proteins are also available from animal sources such as meat, poultry and offal but some of these are high in fat content.

The amount of energy required by you depends on your lifestyle, circumstances and ambitions. If you are a particularly active person your system will require more fuel than a colleague who does not carry out any physical activity. Babies gain about 50 per cent of their energy from fat and have no say in the matter. By comparison, adults can control their food intake and should strive to have a balanced diet.

What is a balanced diet? What are the recommended percentage gains of energy from carbohydrates, fats, and proteins? How do I know what energy giving nutrients are within the products that I consume? These questions are best answered by a nutritionist who would study your lifestyle and circumstances in some detail before replying. However, if you follow some general guidelines and consider your nutritional needs for badminton before, during and after the event, at least you will be helping your system to cope with the demands that are placed upon it.

Healthy adults are recommended to gain 45 to 50 per cent of their energy from carbohydrates, 35 per cent from fat and the remainder from proteins. Athletes need a higher percentage of fuel (about 60 per cent) from carbohydrates, and a reduced amount from fats. An increase in protein intake aids recovery from injury.

MEASURING ENERGY

Energy expended and consumed is measured in kilocalories (kcal) or kilojoules (kj). The amount of energy gained from 1g of pure carbohydrate, fat or protein is as follows:

1g of carbohydrate	4kcal
1g of fat	9kcal
1g of protein	4kcal

It is possible to obtain the overall energy value of different foods if you know what quantities are present. Nowadays this information is frequently written on the packaging and it is therefore possible to work out what percentage of energy is being supplied by each of the three nutrients.

It is possible to compare the contents of 100g of a chocolate wafer bar and 100g of a shredded wheat breakfast cereal. The percentage of energy gained from the nutrients in the chocolate bar are: carbohydrates 47 per cent, fats 47 per cent, protein 6 per cent. The percentage of energy gained from the nutrients in the shredded wheat are: carbohydrates 81 per cent, fats 6 per cent, protein 13 per cent. Therefore, of the two examples, the complex carbohydrate shredded wheat is by far the healthier option.

Fluids

Water provides the means of transporting nutrients around the body and plays an important role in body temperature regulation. For sportsmen a regular intake of fluid is necessary to replace what has been lost during periods of high activity.

Dehydration is a major cause of fatigue that can adversely affect your performance and also be dangerous.

We are bombarded with an over-abundance of information regarding suitable commercial drinks. Hypertonic drinks are loaded with carbohydrates – sometimes as much as 20 per cent – but your system has to draw on water from within the body to assist the digestion process. Isotonic and hypotonic drinks contain much less in carbohydrates and are ideal for competitors in that they provide the body with some carbohydrates but do not need to call on body fluid for the digestion process.

An ideal hypotonic drink example is 250ml of fruit juice mixed with 750ml of water and a pinch of salt. It is important to drink plenty of fluid before you train, small amounts during the event and remember to take in plenty of fluid after training. Do not wait until you feel thirsty before taking a drink.

Before, During and After a Tournament

Stock up on complex carbohydrates before the event.

- Rehearse your eating habits during training to find out what foods suit you
- Do not try to eat anything new
- Increase your fluid intake
- Eat your last meal 3 to 4 hours prior to the event

Foods can be assigned a glycaemic index. Those with a low index are absorbed slowly into the system. During a badminton tournament, assuming that you are progressing through the early rounds, you should try to take in food with a high index little and often. Some examples of high index foods are bananas, tinned fruit in natural juice, yoghurt, cereal bars and currant buns. Drink little amounts at frequent intervals.

Ideally you should replenish your system with food and drink as soon as possible after the competition, which is usually the one time when you do not feel like anything to eat! If the tournament continues the next day, a hearty meal that is high in complex carbohydrates – such as pizza, noodles, rice, pasta or jacket potatoes – is recommended together with plenty of non-alcoholic fluid.

Useful Addresses

International Badminton Federation 4 Manor Park, Mackenzie Way, Cheltenham, Gloucestershire GL51 9TX (telephone 01242 234904). They are the regulating body for the international game and their official magazine is *World Badminton*, published six times a year.

BADMINTON England. The National Governing Body for the game in England.
The National Badminton Centre, Bradwell Road, Loughton Lodge, Milton Keynes MK8 9LA, tel: 01908 268400, email: enquiries@badmintonengland.co.uk . Website: www.badmintonengland.co.uk. The official magazine, BE, is published six times a year. BADMINTON England also produce an annual handbook in which details of County Badminton Associations, Articles of Association, Child Protection and Equal Opportunities Policies are printed.

INDEX